Poems of Goethe

UNC | COLLEGE OF ARTS AND SCIENCES
Germanic and Slavic Languages and Literatures

From 1949 to 2004, UNC Press and the UNC Department of Germanic & Slavic Languages and Literatures published the UNC Studies in the Germanic Languages and Literatures series. Monographs, anthologies, and critical editions in the series covered an array of topics including medieval and modern literature, theater, linguistics, philology, onomastics, and the history of ideas. Through the generous support of the National Endowment for the Humanities and the Andrew W. Mellon Foundation, books in the series have been reissued in new paperback and open access digital editions. For a complete list of books visit www.uncpress.org.

Poems of Goethe

A Sequel to *Goethe, the Lyrist*

NEW TRANSLATIONS FACING THE ORIGINALS, WITH

AN INTRODUCTION AND A LIST OF MUSICAL

SETTINGS BY

EDWIN H. ZEYDEL

UNC Studies in the Germanic Languages and Literatures
Number 20

Copyright © 1957

This work is licensed under a Creative Commons CC BY-NC-ND license. To view a copy of the license, visit http://creativecommons.org/licenses.

Suggested citation: Zeydel, Edwin H. *Poems of Goethe: A Sequel to Goethe, the Lyrist.* Chapel Hill: University of North Carolina Press, 1957. DOI: https://doi.org/10.5149/9781469658698_Zeydel

Library of Congress Cataloging-in-Publication Data
Names: Zeydel, Edwin H.
Title: Poems of Goethe : A sequel to Goethe, the "Lyrist" / by Edwin H. Zeydel.
Other titles: University of North Carolina Studies in the Germanic Languages and Literatures ; no. 20.
Description: Chapel Hill : University of North Carolina Press, [1957] Series: University of North Carolina Studies in the Germanic Languages and Literatures.
Identifiers: LCCN 57062834 | ISBN 978-1-4696-5868-1 (pbk: alk. paper) | ISBN 978-1-4696-5869-8 (ebook)
Classification: LCC PD25 .N6 NO. 20 | DCC 831/ .69

CONTENTS

	Page
Preface	xi
Introduction	1
Some Musical Settings to the Poems	15

Chapter I. Early Poems
1. Zueignung (Dedication) 18
2. Wechsel (Change) 18
3. Stirbt der Fuchs, so gilt der Balg (Dead Fox, Good Hide) 20
4. Ich komme bald (You Precious Children) 20
5. Wanderers Sturmlied (Wanderer's Storm Song) 22
6. Mahomets Gesang (Mahomet's Song) 28
7. Harzreise im Winter (Winter Journey to the Harz Mountains) 32

Chapter II. From "Wilhelm Meister"
1. Mignon 1 40
2. Mignon 2 40
3. Philine 40

Chapter III. Italy
1-2. Römische Elegien X, XVII (Roman Elegies X, XVII) 46
3-6. Epigramme. Venedig 1790, 5, 8, 10, 96 (Venetian Epigrams, 5, 8, 10, 96) 46-48

Chapter IV. Poems of Maturity
1. Alexis und Dora 52
2. Die Braut von Korinth (The Bride of Corinth) 60
3. Mächtiges Überraschen (Mighty Surprise) 70
4. Die Liebende abermals (The Girl Writes Again to her Lover) 70
5. Epoche (Epoch) 72
6. Gleich und gleich (Like and Like) 72
7. Krittler (Fault Finder) 74
8. Poesie (Poetry) 74
9. Urworte. Orphisch (Primal Words. Orphic) 74
10. März (March) 78

Chapter V. From the "West-Easterly Divan"
1-2. Talismane (Talismans) 82
3-5. Buch der Sprüche (Book of Sayings) 82
6. Suleika 1 82
7. Hatem 84
8. Suleika 2 86
9. Suleika 3 86
10. Wiederfinden (Rediscovery) 86
11. Vollmondnacht (Full Moon Night) 90
12. Die Welt durchaus (The World is Fair to View) 90
13. In welchem Weine (What Brand of Wine) 92

Contents

Page

Chapter VI. Late Poems and Epigrams
  1. Parabase (Parabasis) 96
  2. Epirrhema 96
  3. Antepirrhema 96
  4. Ultimatum 98
  5-7. Trilogie der Leidenschaft (Trilogy of Passion)
     1. An Werther (To Werther) 98
     2. Elegie (Elegy) 100
     3. Aussöhnung (Reconciliation) 108
  8-20. Sprüche (Epigrams) 111
  21. Freibeuter (Freebooter) 114
  22. Jahr aus, Jahr ein (Year Out, Year In) 114
  23. Dämmrung senkte sich von oben (Twilight from Above) 116
  24. Der Bräutigam (The Betrothed) 116
  25. Vermächtnis (Legacy) 118
  26. Zur Logenfeier des dritten Septembers 1825. Zwischengesang (On the Lodge Celebration of September 3, 1825. Interlude) 120
  27. Schwebender Genius über der Erdkugel (Hovering Genius over the Earth-Sphere) 120

Index of Titles and First Lines 125

Preface

In the volume *Goethe the Lyrist,* published as No. 16 of this series in 1955, it was stated that another collection of Goethe's shorter poems in English would be attempted if it seemed desirable. The response to the earlier volume has been so cordial on the part of reviewers and many others who have spoken or written words of appreciation, that it appeared proper to prepare the present volume, with emphasis upon the later lyrical output of the poet which is less known in the English-speaking world. Over one-half of the poems here presented are from the last twenty years of Goethe's life. The rest fall into the periods 1769-1777 and 1783-1807.

As in the previous volume, an attempt has been made to exhibit Goethe's versatility. The pure lyric and the thought lyric, the ballad and the idyl, the ode and the dithyramb, the epigram and the elegy, the aphorism and the humorous poem, all find a place, with their widely varying meters, rhythms and themes. If the middle years are less copiously represented, it is because they have found a fuller hearing in *Goethe the Lyrist.*

The principles of translation laid down in the previous volume —careful attention to details of substance, form and style, and to the spirit of the original, as well as simplicity and naturalness of language, so characteristic of Goethe—have been observed in the present volume, too. The feminine rhymes, of which Goethe is very fond, have been retained insofar as it was felt that the genius of the English language would tolerate them. The judicious remarks "On Translating Feminine Rhymes" by Bayard Quincy Morgan in *"On Romanticism and the Art of Translation,* Studies in Honor of Edwin Hermann Zeydel," edited by Gottfried F. Merkel, Princeton University Press for the University of Cincinnati, 1956, pp. 163 ff., have been kept constantly in mind. The German originals again face the translations, and the Introduction aims to serve as a running commentary on the poems.

The slight debt which these new renderings owe to predecessors can be summed up briefly. I, 2, 5, 6, 7, also **IV**, 1 and 6 are indebted in very small degree to Bowring. **II**, 1 and 2 owe one rhyme each to Ludwig Lewisohn's *Goethe, the Story of a*

Man (New York, 1949, I, 296 and 400), while **IV**, 5 is in a small way beholden both to Lewisohn and to Bayard Q. Morgan's rendering of one stanza in Karl Viëtor's *Goethe the Poet* (Cambridge, Mass., 1949, 169). **IV**, 2 owes a slight debt to Aytoun-Martin; **VI**, 6 to Charles Tomlinson in the Oxford edition of *Goethe's Poems and Aphorisms,* edited by Friedrich Bruns (New York, 1932), and to Morgan in the Viëtor volume. **VI**, 16 and 26 are similarly indebted to Morgan in Viëtor.

For the references to musical compositions, sketchy as they necessarily are, I have used the lists of Willi Schuh in vol. II of the *Goethe Gedenkausgabe* (Zürich, 1949), edited by Ernst Beutler, pp. 665 ff., although Schuh is guilty of serious omissions (e.g. Ethelbert Nevin) and pays no attention to opus and number.

As in *Goethe the Lyrist,* my introduction is again indebted to Clarence W. Eastman's *Goethe's Poems* (New York, 1941) and to Barker Fairley's *Goethe, Selected Poems* (New York, 1955). In addition, Karl Viëtor's book, referred to above, has been used to advantage, as have Boyd's *Notes.*

This will be my last attempt to present shorter poems of Goethe to English-speaking readers. After much thought four poems were omitted for special reasons. "Ilmenau" (1783) on the birthday of Duke Karl August, was left out because of its length and rather biographical character. "Der neue Pausias," on the advantage of the painter over the poet in reproducing sensual life; "Euphrosyne" on the lawless caprice of death; and "Amyntas," Goethe's reply to those who criticised him for taking Christiane as his common-law wife—all of 1797-1798—were discarded because they would have weighed down the volume with too many elegiac distichs.

Again I hope that my efforts will serve to bring Goethe, the lyric poet, a little closer to English-speaking readers.

EDWIN H. ZEYDEL

January, 1957

Introduction

When in 1748 the classical period of German literature was ushered in with the appearance of the first three cantos of Klopstock's *Messiah,* German poetry knew only two major types, the abstruse religious or philosophical poem and the ponderous lyric which echoed the elevated tone of the classical ode. Klopstock, the representative of sentimentality and exaltation, not only carried on this tradition but brought it to its climax. He never overcame it, although he did not die until 1803, when in his seventy-ninth year. Today his name lives chiefly in reference books and anthologies. Among the few of his shorter poems generally found there is "The Bond of Roses" (*Das Rosenband*). Its deep feeling and airiness, a singular quality of abstractness that makes it seem unreal and devoid of any basis of experience, are quite typical of its author and his times.

> I found Her in the shade of spring;
> I bound Her fast with bonds of roses:
> She felt it not and slumbered on.
>
> I looked at Her; my life now hung
> On Hers with this one glance I gave her:
> I felt it, yet I knew it not.
>
> With lisping tongue I spoke no word
> And rustled with the bonds of roses:
> With this She wakened from Her sleep.
>
> She looked at me; Her life now hung
> On mine with this one glance she gave me,
> And round us dawned Elysium.[1]

Goethe, four years old when this was written, grew up in an age when such verse was still admired in Germany. He too was attracted to the master, and indeed learned much from him, especially diction, in which Klopstock was an innovator. But what a vast difference, even in Goethe's early poems of the late 'sixties, still under the spell of the rococo style! This difference

---

[1] Im Frühlingsschatten fand ich Sie; / Da band ich Sie mit Rosenbändern: / Sie fühlt' es nicht, und schlummerte. // Ich sah Sie an; mein Leben hing / Mit diesem Blick an Ihrem Leben: / Ich fühlt' es wohl und wusst' es nicht. // Doch lispelt' ich Ihr sprachlos zu / Und rauschte mit den Rosenbändern: / Da wachte Sie vom Schlummer auf. // Sie sah mich an; Ihr Leben hing / Mit diesem Blick an meinem Leben, / Und um uns ward's Elysium.

lies above all in his freedom from abstractness; his reliance upon concrete experience; his novel art of writing poems which do not *describe* experiences, but rather *are* experiences exhibiting the man;[2] his genuineness; and his closeness to nature. Moreover, Klopstock remains ever on the more elevated, ecstatic plane, Goethe, though at home in this too, is, like Pushkin, most impressive when his language is most effortlessly simple and colloquial. His striking new coinages seem no less instinctively achieved than the effects of his homeliest colloquialisms. As Barker Fairley says in the introduction to his recent anthology, *Goethe, Selected Poems* (1955) : "So unartificially does he write that we forget he is writing. It is like the miracle of living, which is there all the time, and we take it for granted." In keeping with the dictum of Keats, Goethe's poetry comes as naturally as leaves come to a tree.

Chapter I.

The first two poems in this chapter, like those in Chapter I of *Goethe the Lyrist*, appeared in the collection of twenty "New Songs" (*Neue Lieder*) set to music by Bernhard Theodor Breitkopf and published by the Breitkopf firm in 1769 (dated Leipzig, 1770). They reflect his love affair with Anna Katharina Schönkopf during his student days in Leipzig (1765-68) and while still revealing signs of adolescence, possess his personal touch. The frivolous pose characteristic of eighteenth-century Anacreontic poets and here still evident, soon disappeared under the Storm and Stress which he experienced in the 'seventies.

1, addressed to the young people of his own generation, was placed at the end of the group in the Breitkopf collection and serves as the key to the twenty poems. Written in 1768 or 1769, these verses reveal the young poet's wariness of the binding ties of matrimony—a feeling which he never quite overcame. At every stage of his life he wrote "unlabored, artless songs." The story of the fox who had lost his tail and tried to make his fellows believe that this was stylish, refers to a fable of Friedrich von Hagedorn, one of the most spirited of the early eighteenth-century poets. 2, one of Goethe's best and most elegant pre-Sesenheim poems, seems clearly to be a reminiscence of his Kätchen Schönkopf affair, written in the light, frivolous mood of the period. The text was revised for later editions.

[2] See Sigurd Burckhardt in *The Germanic Review* XXXI, 1, 35 ff.

3 and 4 reflect the happy visits to the village of Sesenheim, near Strassburg, in 1770-71, where Goethe fell in love with Friederike Brion, the daughter of the village parson. Both poems refer to merry social games in which Goethe participated with the other young folk in Sesenheim. However, neither poem was published at the time, 3 not appearing until 1875 and 4 in 1798. The authorship of 3, at first questioned, is now definitely fixed. 4, referred to by Goethe reminiscently in conversation with Eckermann, his Boswell, as late as 1828, alludes to a social game, still known in Bowring's England as "Jack's alight" (see also Goethe's letter to Riemer of May 4, 1807). The company would sit in a circle, while a glimmering taper was passed from hand to hand, each one, on receiving it, reciting a nonsense verse of six lines and then passing the taper on. The one in whose hand the ember died paid a forfeit. The name "Dorilis" is typical for pastoral poetry.

5 and 6, written in 1772 and 1773, respectively, betray the change that had come over the poet in the brief span of a year or two, chiefly under the influence of Rousseau's writings and Herder's teachings. Effervescent revolt against tradition and reason, emphasis upon the emotional, intuitive, imaginative side of man, advocacy of primitivism, delight in Nature, and protest against authority and social conventions are the principal characteristics of his new "Storm and Stress" view of life.

In 5 "Storm and Stress," or the "Age of the Genius," as it was called, erupts violently and with dithyrambic ardor. Later Goethe himself called the poem half nonsense, but it is *meaningful* nonsense. Although its middle section is weak and the ending anticlimactic, it compares favorably with "Prometheus" (III, 2 in *Goethe the Lyrist*). The mire through which the genius-inspired wanderer walks—Goethe's own morose mood and his humdrum life in Frankfurt after returning from Strassburg—is compared with the mud which confronted Deucalion, the classical Noah, when Apollo slew the serpent Python. Then the poet, braving the hail and snow and fired by his own genial poetic glow, compares himself with the peasant who looks forward only to a warming fire and a bottle of spirits, symbolized by the god Bromius, who is boisterous Dionysus, the Century's Genius. This comparison cheers the poet because *he* is inspired by the Muses and Graces. He praises Jupiter Pluvius, the god of the storm and rain, whose deluging torrents make the Castalian fount on Parnassus, in which less virile poets rejoice, seem like a brooklet at one side. Bowing to Anacreon, "the dallying poet happy with flowers," and Theocritus, "singing of bees," and passing by the wealth and luxury of the ancient town of Sybaris, he allies himself with Pindar, the foremost of the Greek lyric poets. Through his own inner glow he even sends a little light towards Phoebus Apollo, but hopes that the sungod may not envy him, as he does the ever green cedars which thrive without the sun. In the last five lines the poet comes back to earth, disillusioned because the fire within him is not as potent as he had dreamed. Nevertheless the total impression he leaves is one of exultant faith in life.

6 is easier to follow. Again in free rhythms, it depicts the rush of a mountain stream devouring the smaller brooks and freshets, its brothers, until, as a lordly river, it empties into Father Ocean. As in "Song of the Spirits over the Waters" (*Goethe the Lyrist* IV, 4), a deeper symbolic meaning is involved. The stream, like a prophet, leads his "brothers" on to join the Father, who produced them all. Originally intended as part of an unfinished drama *Mahomet*, it was meant to be an antiphonal song in praise of the prophet, sung by Ali, his devotee, and Fatema, the prophet's daughter. The present title, now misleading, dates from 1777. A pendant to this poem is to be found in the sonnet "Mighty Surprise" (IV, 3), where, however, the stream (and the poet) are arrested in their progress to the Father by the Greek nymph Oreas (passion) and dammed to form a lake.

7 is a rhapsody written in 1777 on a solitary winter excursion to the Harz mountains and its highest peak, the Brocken. It is too often missing in anthologies, considering that Brahms uses the middle section in his "Alto Rhapsody," and Rainer Maria Rilke was drawn closer to Goethe by it. Like the vulture, Goethe's creative urge is looking for prey. After an introduction on human happiness and fate, three sections describe: 1) the prince and courtiers on a hunt; 2) a recluse who has turned to hating his fellows (Goethe had a young man in mind whose milk of human kindness had been soured by the reading of *Werther*); and 3) the poet who, though also alone, is in "clouds of gold"—the darling of Love envisaged under various aspects. He prays for the others as well as himself while ascending the mountain, the scene of the witches' sabbath (the

spirit-dances) on the night before Mayday. The poem ends with an apostrophe of the Brocken, which Goethe climbed in December of that year. Here he surrenders to the deity, who is sublimely distant but "mysteriously revealed," like the summit of the mountain. Goethe also sketched a mediocre drawing of the Brocken. In 1797 this mountain became the scene of his "Walpurgis Night" in *Faust I*; in 1821 he wrote a special commentary on the poem; and in the "Campaign in France" (*Campagne in Frankreich*), written in 1822 in reminiscence of the campaign in which he participated as a disinterested neutral with Duke Karl August in 1792, he touches upon the journey once more.

Chapter II.

Biographically, there is a gap of about six years between this chapter and I. It is covered by Chapters III and IV of the earlier volume, *Goethe the Lyrist*. The present work aims to stress the later periods of the poet's life. In Chapter II we pass on to three songs from the novel *Wilhelm Meister*, begun in 1777, perhaps earlier. 1 and 2, well suited to the romantic aura surrounding the character of Mignon, a poor waif (in reality the daughter of the Harper, who turns out to be a nobleman), were probably written in 1783 and are already found in the earlier draft of the novel, broken off in 1786. Before singing 1, Mignon had had a vision of the Virgin Mary, who promised to take her under her tutelage. The reference is to Mignon's vow that she would entrust to no one the secret of her origin (if indeed she knew it herself). She compares her secret to the night, which will ultimately be paled by the sun, and to the cliff which will open its recesses and gush forth hidden waters. 2, again a monolog of Mignon, alludes to her love for Wilhelm, the hero. Up to this point she had preferred boys' clothing, but now at a birthday party she appears among the children in a white gown, golden girdle, diadem, and wings, to distribute gifts. The children address her as an angel. 3 was written for the later final version of the novel in 1795. Philine, a young actress and friend of Wilhelm, is as charming as she is lighthearted, as loyal as she is unscrupulous. Her paean on the joys of the nighttime, though not very profound, may be associated with the *Night Thoughts* of Edward Young and with similar sentiments of the German romanticists, especially Novalis. Such haunting music as that of the *Wilhelm Meister* songs was rarely achieved again by Goethe or any of his successors.

Chapter III.

Turning from the songs of *Wilhelm Meister* to the poems written in, or inspired by, Italy during his two visits (1786-1788 and 1790), we are immediately impressed by Goethe's versatility as a poet. As his models he now adopts the Roman elegiac poet, Propertius, in the Roman Elegies, and the satirical writer of epigrams, Martial, in the Venetian Epigrams. Both groups are composed in elegiac couplets, the Roman Elegies partly during his first stay in Italy and partly during the next two years in Weimar. There are twenty-four Elegies. Twenty were published for the first time in Schiller's periodical, *Die Horen,* in 1795; the others, more erotic than the rest, were not definitively printed until 1914 in the Weimar edition. The lady involved may well be a composite of Faustina Antonini, a widow whose acquaintance he made in Rome, other Italian beauties, and Christiane Vulpius, his common-law-wife-to-be, whom he met in Weimar in 1788. The sensuous love of these Elegies is the uninhibited expression of rapturous carnal pleasure characteristic of the ancients.

Quite different in nature are the 103 Venetian Epigrams of 1790 reflecting in part at least his second, briefer Italian voyage, this time only to Venice. It was marred by disappointment and bad weather. Nostalgia and longing for Christiane crop up in these poems (see our No. 6). They contain acid, vermouth, and salt but mostly lack the eroticism and pleasant personal touch of the Elegies.

Chapter IV.

This chapter comprises ten poems from the middle years of Goethe's life, when both rococo and Storm and Stress lay far behind him, and the maturing influence of Italy and its classical associations had clarified his art. 1 was written and published in 1796, during a period when the hexameter and the elegiac distich of antiquity still teased his mind and tempted him again and again to fuse ancient form with modern content. The heroine of the elegy is named for Dora Stock, the sister-in-law of Christian G. Körner, who with the Körners was visiting Schiller in Jena at the time. Goethe remembered the Stock sisters from his Leipzig days, when their father had instructed him in engraving. Goethe biographers, always in search for links between the poet's life and his poetry, have mentioned Christiane, who sometimes aroused mild jealousy in him, and a Milanese beauty, Maddalena Riggi, as also involved in this idyl. The latter, it appears, attracted Goethe in Italy and requited his affection, but not until the last moments before the final farewell did they exchange assurances of love. The idyl was highly praised by Goethe's friends for its fine diction, simplicity of plot, and depth of feeling, although Schiller was disturbed by the hero's outburst of jealousy at the end. The locale may be the Bay of Naples, and the mood is that of Ovid's *Heroides*. The time is Goethe's own. The entire action may be imagined to take less than an hour, but the "flash-back," in a soliloquy of the lover, gives us a moving account of his belated love. As often in Goethe, joy and grief go hand in hand. Those who like Viëtor interpret the ending as implying Alexis' death, overlook the fact that an idyl by its very nature requires no dénouement.

2 was written in 1797, the "ballad year," in which Goethe and Schiller vied with one another in this form. It should be read in conjunction with "The God and the Bayadere" (*Goethe the Lyrist*, VI, 12). Both poets, under the spell of the "tyranny" of ancient Greece, were intrigued by its pagan mythology and religion. The time of this ballad is that of Christianity in its early stages, when it was slowly displacing the pagan beliefs. The young Athenian, still clinging to the old faith, comes to Corinth to claim his beloved, only to find that her domineering mother has, during a recent siege of illness, embraced the new religion with all its early asceticism. The eerie legend which Goethe uses is that of the animate corpse, or vampire, that entices her lover, still living, to the tomb of death. The naive piety of the ancient Greeks is vividly opposed to what Goethe interprets as the unnatural, jejune asceticism which replaced it and to which Eros succumbed. The meter—four five-beat trochaic lines, followed by two of three beats each, and a single one of again five—effectively underscores the mood of the poem.

The three sonnets which follow (Nos. 3, 4, 5) date from 1807-1808, a period in which Goethe wrote seventeen poems in the Petrarchan form. 3 was probably intended for Minna Herzlieb, an eighteen-year-old foster daughter of the Jena publisher Frommann, whom the poet had already known as a child and with whom he was now in love. It was referred to above, in Chapter

I. No. 5, also addressed to her, refers to their earlier friendship. Already interested in the Petrarchan sonnet as a form at the beginning of the century (see VI, 21, in *Goethe the Lyrist*), Goethe turned to it with renewed zest in 1807, when Frommann published an edition of Petrarch. During this year Bettina, the sister of the romantic poet Clemens Brentano, who four years later married Achim von Arnim, her brother's friend and collaborator on the folk-song collection, "The Boy's Cornucopia" (*Des Knaben Wunderhorn*), visited Goethe in Weimar twice. A sprightly and charming but aggressive maiden, she was smitten with the fifty-eight-year-old poet, somewhat to his embarrassment. About half a dozen of his sonnets may have been evoked by her and sent to her in letters. Her later statement in her rather imaginative book, "Goethe's Correspondence with a Child" (*Goethes Briefwechsel mit einem Kind*), 1835, that nine of them, including our No. 3, were addressed to her, is exaggerated. No. 4 at any rate, seems actually to have been written for her. 3 and 4 were first published in 1815, 5 later.

6 shows that even at sixty-four Goethe was still capable of "unlabored, artless songs." It appears the first time in a letter of April, 1814, to his friend, the composer Zelter. 7 shows Goethe's humorous, satiric vein just as fresh in 1815 as it was in 1774, when he paid his respects to the critics of that day (*Goethe the Lyrist* III, 12).

8, 9, and 10, written in 1816 and 1817, were all published in the collection of studies which came out under the title "On Art and Antiquity" (*Über Kunst und Altertum*), a series of reports on the art treasures, both public and private, found in various centers of Germany. 8 pays homage to the humanizing and civilizing qualities of art, while 10 again shows Goethe setting his hand to an older song, this one by an unnamed poet of the fifteenth or sixteenth century (see also *Goethe the Lyrist* II, 2; VI, 13, 15; IX, 5).

9, though by no means the first of Goethe's philosophical poems, is one of the best of his "years that bring the philosophic mind," as Wordsworth puts it. It was originally published as separate stanzas, which were obviously meant to form a unit from the beginning. Though related to Platonic philosophy, they profess to revert to the pre-Homeric "Orphic" cosmogony or mysteries of the Greeks, said to be traceable to older Egyptian ideas, which saw in the gods Demon, Chance, Love and Necessity (to whom Goethe adds Hope) powers that ally themselves with every new-born child. In a four-page commentary to the poem Goethe explains that he meant to re-interpret these forces, or charms, in the light of his own experiences. They might more clearly be re-named innate personality, environment, passion or emotion, destiny, and hope borne by imagination.

In the first stanza he comes back to the principle which he saw at work in the hero of his drama *Egmont,* and which he later depicts in the last book of his autobiography "Poetry and Truth" (*Dichtung und Wahrheit*). It develops not from astrological barbarism, but from the conviction that each individual is created unique and cannot elude the stamp which nature has given him—his demon, as Heraclitus puts it, which drives him.

In the second stanza the factor of chance, of environmental circumstances affecting the individual favorably or unfavorably, is introduced—the conditions into which he chances to be born and with which he must come to grips. Then in the third, Eros, or emotion, emerges from chaos and links demon and chance. It makes man conscious of his free will and choice, laying the groundwork for marriage, family, and community. Here the noble personality, unlike the baser individual, will not dissipate his loyalty and love, but practice concentration.

In the fourth stanza grim fate in the guise of law sets bounds to man's delusive self-will, so that he must accept the inevitable and arrive at renunciation. Finally, in the last stanza, Goethe introduces his own often invoked deity of hope buttressed by imagination. No man can live without it. It unlocks the future and leaves the legion of fleeting years behind. Thus Goethe's five charms, opposing yet complementing each other, dominate man's life and its various periods. Only the spring of hope endures in his breast. Religion in the accepted sense, however, is ignored.

Chapter V.

The incomplete twelve-book collection of partly proverbial, partly love poems which Goethe wrote in 1814-1815, after five years of comparative unproductiveness, and published as "West-Easterly Divan" (*Der west-östliche Divan*) in 1819, was meant to amalgamate Western and Eastern, or German and Persian, philosophies. It was chiefly the result of his interest in the religions and wisdom of the East, in Mohammed and the Koran, study, in poor translations, of Persian and other Eastern authors, particularly the *Divan* of the fourteenth-century poet Hafis, and the untoward political conditions prevailing in Germany at that time, from which Goethe wished to escape. Marianne von Willemer, a lovely and intelligent Austrian girl, now married in Frankfurt, who was herself the author of several of the poems, played the part of Suleika—a character in the Koran—to Goethe's Hatem or Hatim, an Arabian poet, in a romantic give and take. But he did not meet her until after he had begun the work.

The two Talismans, 1 and 2—the other three are in *Goethe the Lyrist*—, appear in the "Book of the Singer." 3, 4, and 5 are from the "Book of Sayings." 6-12 come from the "Book of Suleika," the richest of the entire work. 6, a jocose dialog between the two lovers, glorifies man's personality in the light and warmth of the aging poet's love and introduces one of his favorite ideas, the constant rebirth of man as an expression of a natural life process (see *Goethe the Lyrist* VIII, 6). Ferdusi (properly Firdausi) was the greatest epic poet of Persia, who died in 1020, while Montanabbi, the "prophet pretender," refers to the tenth-century poet Ab't Taijib Achmed ibn Hosain, who compared himself with Mohammed.

In Goethe's clean copy of the Divan collection 7 and 8 appear together on a single sheet, dated September 30, 1815. The hilltops in 7 refer to the heights behind the Heidelberg castle. Lines 1-3 of stanza 3 in the original, it will be noted, lack rhyme (-röte—Hatem)—a sly trick of Goethe, who thus suggests his own name in the place of Hatem's. 8, with its memorable last lines, has usually been attributed to Marianne, but recent research, summed up and supplemented by Kurt Keppler's article in *Modern Language Notes* LXX, June, 1955, 433-437, makes it clear that it was the work of Goethe. 9 was actually written by Marianne late in September, 1815. In the poetry of Hafis the East wind is the harbinger of love, and dust is often mentioned, too. Goethe revised stanzas 4 and 5, to her and our dissatisfaction. 10 was written by Goethe at the same time, placed in a later collection, and then restored to the "Divan." The first and last stanzas apply directly to him and Marianne, while the rest of the poem offers a picture of Creation, with the planets and all the elements in mad confusion, until God created light and the colors of the prism. This led to love and harmony, which made it possible for the elective affinities to seek each other out. In the form of evolution this process of creation continues to the present day, Goethe avers. The middle portion is closely linked with the first and last stanzas. As in 6 above, the individual personality or *ego* can come to full fruition only when complemented by a *tu* or thou. As Viëtor puts it, "the pulse-beat of the world is the desire of the separated for union with the whole, for each individualized thing evolves from an entity which distributes itself in polar opposites, only for each then to reunite with its complementary counterpart." Allah is identified here with God. 10 is a pendant to "Blissful Yearning" (*Selige Sehnsucht*) ; see *Goethe the Lyrist* VIII, 6.

11, written late in October, 1815, as a reply to a letter of Marianne, is a dialog between a female slave and her mistress, the slave revealing the situation and the mistress dwelling only upon her desire to kiss her lover. The change in tense in the final line is striking. Goethe and Marianne, now separated, had actually vowed to think of one another at the time of full moon. 12, written in February, 1815, is to be associated with the numerous other poems in which Goethe stresses the visual sensations. See the final poem in the present collection and IX, 22 in *Goethe the Lyrist*. First published a few years after Goethe's death, 13 is found in the remains, or *Nachlass*, of the "Divan," wine being a symbol for the poet's noblest aspirations.

Chapter VI.

Except for a few aphorisms, all the poems in this chapter date from the 'twenties, when Goethe was a septuagenarian. The selection is purposely wide enough to show that even then his awareness was not confined to philosophy and wisdom. He roamed widely from man, nature, and love to mere banter. 1-3 are found in a work on morphology. 1—the title refers to a choral ode on personal or state matters in Old Greek comedy— expresses a belief basic to Goethe's attitude toward nature, *viz.* that each individual specimen, according to its species, is a divergent but related variation of a prototype, a manifestation of "the eternal One and All." 2 and 3, whose technical headings describe discourses of the leader of the chorus in Greek Comedy, dwell upon a closely related theme: that internal element and external form are inseparable because idea and individual specimen, or type and phenomenon, are coordinate. To Goethe these are "open mysteries." Eternal truth and phenomenon, solemnity and seeming playfulness are but evidence of the One Idea in its manifold occurrences. In 3 the figure of the loom serves as a graphic illustration. See *Faust* I, 501 ff. and 1922 ff. In 4, as in another poem of these years inscribed "To be sure" (*Allerdings*), Goethe opposes a widespread notion of the eighteenth century that man cannot penetrate the inner secrets of Nature, and indeed, is scarcely able to get to her outer shell.

5-7 constitute one of Goethe's most famous lyrical works. Although written in the reverse order (7-5) between August, 1823, and March, 1824, they should be read in their present sequence. They became a trilogy by chance, their central burden being the violent Indian Summer love of the seventy-four-year-old poet for Ulrike von Levetzow, a girl of nineteen, whom he had met in the summer of 1821 in Bohemia and fallen desperately in love with two summers later. For a while he seriously contemplated marriage, a thought which both Ulrike and her mother, but not Goethe's friend and ruler, the Grand Duke, rejected.

6 with its Byronic qualities was written September, 1823, in Goethe's coach, while returning to Weimar after his final farewell from Ulrike in Karlsbad, Bohemia. In Marienbad and since the latter part of August, in Karlsbad, Goethe had spent a wonderful summer of rejuvenation with Ulrike, taking part in excursions, social affairs, and dances. Despite the renunciation expressed in 6, the poet still hoped against hope until November, when a brief but serious psychosomatic illness overtook him. The motto varies the last soliloquy in the drama *Torquato Tasso*, 3432 f. An interval of a few days should be assumed between stanzas 1 and 2; the last two stanzas also are to be set off. Stanzas 2 and 3 refer to the happy days in Marienbad, when he had rooms in the same house with the Levetzows. In stanza 6, as in the next to the last, he is thinking of solace in nature, especially in the study of meteorology and cloud formation. His coachman and secretary had helped him during that summer in overcoming emotional crises through scientific pursuits. The ungrammatical form "lastest" (stanza 9), also used in *Faust* II and comparable to Shakespeare's "most unkindest," is impressive in this context. The reference to God's peace in stanza 13 alludes to St. Paul's Epistle to the Philippians 4, 7. This and the next stanza are perhaps the finest in the elegy. The poet's very being is stirred by sacred emotions, which

transport him into the realm of religion. It is now not passion, but supreme love which contemplates the divine in beautiful human form, as Viëtor points out. The words of comfort put into Ulrike's mouth in stanzas 16 and 17 are of course thoughts of Goethe himself. The spectacle of the aged man giving vent to his tears in stanza 19, and his utter dejection in 20, take the poem to a new climax, which permits no hope, even at the end. In stanza 21 he admits that the very thought of being without his beloved is alien to him, nor does he find solace in Pandora in the final stanza (a name he also gave to Ulrike's mother in his diary), the "all-gifted," whose box, according to Goethe's version, contained all good and evil which scattered over the earth, leaving only hope. In 1810 Goethe wrote a play *Pandora*, a symbolic myth in Plato's style.

5 was written in March, 1824, as an introduction to a golden jubilee edition of the novel "The Sorrows of Young Werther" (*Die Leiden des jungen Werthers*) and sets the tone of the trilogy. The pessimism of the last couplet of stanza 1, and of stanza 2, is unusual for Goethe. In stanza 3 the magic of "the Eternal Womanly" breaks all barriers, only to be frustrated by the grief of separation. The final line leads directly to the motto and mood of **6**.

7, written the middle of August, 1823, shortly after the Levetzows had departed from Marienbad, expresses the alleviation to the poet's wounded heart (actually not yet achieved at that time), brought about by the artistry of Maria Szymanowska, a Polish pianiste, whom Goethe met in Marienbad. "O would it ever be like this!" sounds once more the dominant note of the Elegy, here expressed in a conciliatory mood.

8-20, like IX, 8-17 in *Goethe the Lyrist*, offer epigrams and aphorisms, a form in which Goethe was very prolific in his later years. 8-10, 14-17, and 19 are found in the so-called "Tame Xenia" (*Zahme Xenien*, 1820-1827), while the rest were written between 1815 and 1827. 21 and 22 show the poet in a playful mood as late as 1827. The freebooter, or buccaneer, of 21, is even at odds with grammar!

23 is from the short cycle "Chinese-German Seasons and Days" (*Chinesisch-Deutsche Jahres- und Tageszeiten*), 1827, a reflection of Goethe's dabbling in Chinese literature in German translation. Again we note his visual perception, even of the coolness of the night, and his sensitiveness to the slightest

stirring in nature. 24, like IX, 6 and 7 in *Goethe the Lyrist*, was written at Dornburg castle near Jena, where Goethe retired in 1828 after the death of Grand Duke Karl August. It was meant for Marianne, and is one of his last love poems. He recalls earlier days of love, happy times of longing and fulfilment. Hand in hand the lovers watch the setting sun, hopefully anticipating the new day. Finally, when the old man's midnight has arrived, he muses on the life he has led, and perhaps on a beloved who has preceded him in death. Death, like the setting sun, promises new life—a desirable consummation, since "living, however it may be, is good." Thus the seventy-nine-year-old poet affirms life.

25 is a pendant to "One and All" (*Goethe the Lyrist* IX, 19), in which Goethe had said that the world is not static but is constantly reshaping itself, and that "everything must decay, if it would live to stand the test." The complementary truth opposed to this in 25 is the principle of permanence in change. This, says Goethe, has always been taught by the wisest of the sages (his specific reference in stanza 2 is to Copernicus). Man's own inner cosmos is ordered along similar lines by the Kantian moral law within him. But our sensual perception can be depended upon more than Kant admits, provided our intellect is sound. If we keep our eyes open to the blessings of the earth and of life, if we let reason prevail, practise moderation, and look upon the moment of fulfilment as something which cannot be destroyed by time, we shall be getting the most out of life. "Fruitful things alone are true," says Goethe, the pragmatist. What counts for him is the contribution which truth makes to life. Man, he argues (as Ibsen and Nietzsche did later), must ally himself with "the smallest group"—the minority of thinkers who are often ahead of their time. The philosophers and poets of all ages have created the most imperishable works of truth, which are in reality works of love serving all noble spirits and guides.

Goethe, a member of the Weimar masonic lodge, wrote several songs for the use of his fellow-masons. The best, 26, is the interlude to a longer poem commemorating the fiftieth anniversary of Grand Duke Karl August's assumption of the reins of government. Never did Goethe express more clearly and succinctly the creed which informs the 12,111 lines of his *Faust*.

27, finally, found among his literary remains, was inspired by an allegorical representation of an angel hovering over a globe, with one hand pointing downward toward earth, and the other upward. Two motifs, one the azure distance, which calls forth the colorful world of day and arouses man's zest for earthly life, and the other, the starry sky of night, which brings to mind the infinity of the cosmos, serve to illustrate man's position between time and eternity. He can be truly great if he will grasp these two worlds rationally and emotionally and harmonize them in doing what is right, for such is his supreme destiny as a moral being. This poem, written probably in 1826, but not published until after the poet's death, voices the same rapture in the world of the eye as is found in the "Song of the Tower Keeper" (*Goethe the Lyrist* IX, 22), but is more profound in its expression of supreme truths, voiced by one whose apologia was "for I was a human being, and that means a fighter too" (denn ich bin ein Mensch gewesen, und das heisst ein Kämpfer sein).

* * *

SOME MUSICAL SETTINGS TO THE POEMS

(The numeral in parentheses indicates the total number of settings listed by Schuh)

I, 1. B. T. Breitkopf (1).
   2. B. T. Breitkopf, C. Loewe, J. F. Reichardt (7).
   3. P. Grönland, W. Tomaschek, C. F. Zelter (7).
   4. A. Ursprach (2).
   5. R. Strauss (3).
   6. C. Loewe, C. Reinecke, F. Schubert (two), H. Zilcher (10).
   7. R. Pannwitz, J. Brahms (part), W. Langhans (part), J. F. Reichardt (part) (4).

II, 1. A. v. Radziwill, J. Reichardt, A. Rubinstein, F. Schubert (two), R. Schumann, C. F. Zelter (19).
   2. A. v. Radziwill, J. F. Reichardt, A. Rubinstein, F. Schubert (four), R. Schumann, H. Wolf, C. F. Zelter (24).
   3. A. v. Radziwill, J. F. Reichardt, A. Rubinstein, R. Schumann, H. Wolf (17).

III, 4. E. Pepping, O. Schoeck (2).
    5. E. Pepping (1).

IV, 2. C. Loewe, C. F. Zelter (6), also opera by E. Chabrier.

SOME MUSICAL SETTINGS TO THE POEMS

      6. R. Franz, E. Mac Dowell, C. Reinecke, R. Strauss, H. Wolf, C. F. Zelter (29).
      9. W. Petersen, H. Pfitzner (9).
    10. K. Eberwein, C. Loewe, W. Taubert (39).
V, 7. A. Mendelssohn, H. Wolf (2).
      8. H. Wolf (2).
      9. F. Mendelssohn-Bartholdy, F. Schubert (5).
    10. C. F. Zelter (3).
    11. W. Petersen, H. Werner (4).
    12. A. Moeschinger (born 1897) (1).
VI, 1. O. Kreis, O. Schoeck (2).
   5-6. K. Bleyle (1).
      7. K. Bleyle, G. Böttcher, C. Ehrensperger, T. Kewitsch (13).
      9. R. Kahn (1).
    21. C. Loewe, H. Marschner, W. Taubert (11).
    23. G. Böttcher, J. Brahms, H. Leichtentritt, O. Schoeck (20).
    24. H. Zilcher (3).
    25. Stanza 5: A. Thate (1).
    26. J. N. Hummel, W. Nagel, C. F. Zelter (4).
    27. W. Petersen (1).

Note: In the Appendix to *Goethe the Lyrist*, Haydn, it was incorrectly stated, composed no music to Goethe's lyrics. Beside "Schauspielmusik" to *Götz von Berlichingen* he composed settings to five minor poems, including VI, 14 in *Goethe the Lyrist*.

CHAPTER I. EARLY POEMS

1. ZUEIGNUNG

Da sind sie nun! Da habt ihr sie,
Die Lieder, ohne Kunst und Müh'
Am Rand des Bachs entsprungen!
Verliebt, und jung, und voll Gefühl
Trieb ich der Jugend altes Spiel,
Und hab' sie so gesungen.

Sie singe, wer sie singen mag!
An einem hübschen Frühlingstag
Kann sie der Jüngling brauchen.
Der Dichter blinzt von ferne zu,
Jetzt drückt ihm diätet'sche Ruh
Den Daumen auf die Augen.

Halb scheel, halb weise sieht sein Blick
Ein bisschen nass auf euer Glück
Und jammert in Sentenzen.
Hört seine letzten Lehren an!
Er hat's so gut wie ihr getan
Und kennt des Glückes Grenzen.

Ihr seufzt, und singt, und schmelzt und küsst,
Und jauchzet, ohne dass ihr's wisst,
Dem Abgrund in der Nähe.
Flieht Wiese, Bach und Sonnenschein,
Schleicht, soll's euch wohl im Winter sein,
Bald zu dem Herd der Ehe.

Ihr lacht mich aus und ruft: Der Tor,
Der Fuchs, der seinen Schwanz verlor,
Verschnitt' jetzt gern uns alle!
Doch hier passt nicht die Fabel ganz,
Das treue Füchslein ohne Schwanz
Das warnt euch für der Falle.

2. WECHSEL

Auf Kieseln im Bache da lieg' ich, wie helle!
Verbreite die Arme der kommenden Welle,
Und buhlerisch drückt sie die sehnende Brust.
Dann führt sie der Leichtsinn im Strome darnieder,
Es naht sich die zweite, sie streichelt mich wieder:
So fühl' ich die Freuden der wechselnden Lust.

1. DEDICATION

They're here! I pass them on to you,
Unlabored, artless songs that grew
Along the brook, or near it!
In love, and young, and all aflame
I played young people's ancient game
And sang them in such a spirit.

Now sing the songs whoever may!
On some delightful springtime day
Such songs will please the lover.
The poet from his distant nest
Peers at them while postprandial rest
His eyes with thumbs will cover.

Jealous, half wise, his eyes would leer
At all your joy, and shed a tear
And moan sententious feelings.
O hear his final teaching true!
He's done his task as well as you
And knows luck's fickle dealings.

You sigh and sing and melt and kiss,
And cheer, where ignorance is bliss,
The near pit men disparage.
Flee meadow, brook, and sunshine warm,
And slink, escaping winter's harm,
To seek the hearth of marriage.

You cry, "The fool," and taunt and scoff,
"The fox that had his tail cut off
Would have us amputated!"
But here the fabled teachings pale:
The faithful fox that lost his tail
Warns you: the trap is baited!

2. CHANGE

I lie in the brook, the bright pebbles as pillow,
And open my arms to the oncoming billow.
Coquettish she fondles my languishing breast.
Downstream by frivolity then she is beckoned,
Again I'm caressed by a billow—the second:
With thrills of a change in love thus I am blest.

Und doch, und so traurig, verschleifst du vergebens
Die köstlichen Stunden des eilenden Lebens,
Weil dich das geliebteste Mädchen vergisst!
O ruf sie zurücke, die vorigen Zeiten!
Es küsst sich so süsse die Lippe der Zweiten,
Als kaum sich die Lippe der Ersten geküsst.

3. STIRBT DER FUCHS, SO GILT DER BALG

Nach Mittage sassen wir
Junges Volk im Kühlen,
Amor kam, und **stirbt der Fuchs**
Wollt' er mit uns spielen.

Jeder meiner Freunde sass
Froh bei seinem Herzchen,
Amor blies die Fackel aus,
Sprach: Hier ist das Kerzchen!

Und die Fackel, wie sie glomm,
Liess man eilig wandern,
Jeder drückte sie geschwind
In die Hand des andern.

Und mir reichte Dorilis
Sie mit Spott und Scherze;
Kaum berührt mein Finger sie,
Hell entflammt die Kerze,

Sengt mir Augen und Gesicht,
Setzt die Brust in Flammen,
Über meinem Haupte schlug
Fast die Glut zusammen.

Löschen wollt' ich, patschte zu;
Doch es brennt beständig:
Statt zu sterben, ward der Fuchs
Recht bei mir lebendig.

4. ICH KOMME BALD

Ich komme bald, ihr goldnen Kinder!
Vergebens sperret uns der Winter
In unsre warmen Stuben ein.
Wir wollen uns zum Feuer setzen

And yet you are squandering vainly in sadness
The moments that life, as it flies, gave for gladness
Because by your love you're remembered no more.
Recall them, recall them, the times that have wasted!
As sweet will the kiss of the second have tasted
As scarce any the lips of the first gave before.

3. DEAD FOX, GOOD HIDE

After noon we young folk sat
In the cool, at leisure,
Cupid came to play with us,
"Dead Fox" gave us pleasure.

All my friends were seated there
With their love beside them,
Cupid snuffed our torch and said:
"Here's new light to guide them."

Passing quickly in the round
Went the burning taper,
Pressed by each into the hand
Of his waiting neighbor,

Passed from Dorilis to me,
Half in jest, to spite me;
Scarcely has it touched my hand,
When the flame burns brightly,

Sears my eye and sears my face,
Sets my breast on fire,
Closing in upon my head,
Leaping ever higher.

And I slapped to put it out,
But it burns the harder:
Far from dead, the fox I held
Showed more life and ardor.

4. YOU PRECIOUS CHILDREN

You precious children, soon I'll come!
In vain does winter keep us home,
Confined in heated rooms to stay.
We'll take our seats around the ingle

Und tausendfältig uns ergetzen,
Uns lieben wie die Engelein.
Wir wollen kleine Kränzchen winden,
Wir wollen kleine Sträusschen binden
Und wie die kleinen Kinder sein.

5. WANDERERS STURMLIED

Wen du nicht verlässest, Genius,
Nicht der Regen, nicht der Sturm
Haucht ihm Schauer übers Herz.
Wen du nicht verlässest, Genius,
Wird dem Regengewölk,
Wird dem Schlossensturm
Entgegen singen,
Wie die Lerche,
Du da droben.

Den du nicht verlässest, Genius,
Wirst ihn heben übern Schlammpfad
Mit den Feuerflügeln.
Wandeln wird er
Wie mit Blumenfüssen
Über Deukalions Flutschlamm,
Python tötend, leicht, gross,
Pythius Apollo.

Den du nicht verlässest, Genius,
Wirst die wollnen Flügel unterspreiten,
Wenn er auf dem Felsen schläft,
Wirst mit Hüterfittigen ihn decken
In des Haines Mitternacht.

Wen du nicht verlässest, Genius,
Wirst im Schneegestöber
Warmumhüllen;
Nach der Wärme ziehn sich Musen,
Nach der Wärme Charitinnen.

Umschwebet mich, ihr Musen,
Ihr Charitinnen!
Das ist Wasser, das ist Erde,
Und der Sohn des Wassers und der Erde,
Über den ich wandle
Göttergleich.

And in a thousand pleasures mingle,
And love each other as angels may.
Some little chaplets we will wind us,
Some little nosegays we will bind us,
Like little children found at play.

5. WANDERER'S STORM SONG

Whom you never leave, o Genius,
Neither rain and neither storm
Will breathe shudders across his heart.
Whom you never leave, o Genius,
He'll greet the clouds of rain,
Greet the storms of hail
With cheerful song,
Like you, o lark,
High in the sky.

Whom you never leave, o Genius,
Him you will raise over the mire
With your wings of flame.
He will wander
In a trail of flowers
Over Deucalion's slimy flood,
Python-slaying, light-footed, great,
A Pythian Apollo.

Whom you never leave, o Genius,
Under him you'll spread your downy wings
When he's sleeping on the cliffs,
Put protecting pinions round him
In the midnight of the grove.

Whom you never leave, o Genius,
Him you will wrap warm
In the snow storm;
Warmth is sought by all the Muses,
Warmth is sought by all the Graces.

Hover about me, Muses,
You Graces also!
That is water, that is earth,
And the child of water and of earth
Over whom I travel
Like the gods.

Ihr seid rein, wie das Herz der Wasser,
Ihr seid rein, wie das Mark der Erde,
Ihr umschwebt mich, und ich schwebe
Über Wasser, über Erde,
Göttergleich.

*

Soll der zurückkehren,
Der kleine, schwarze, feurige Bauer?
Soll der zurückkehren, erwartend
Nur deine Gaben, Vater Bromius,
Und helleuchtend umwärmend Feuer?
Der kehren mutig?
Und ich, den ihr begleitet,
Musen und Charitinnen alle,
Den alles erwartet, was ihr,
Musen und Charitinnen,
Umkränzende Seligkeit,
Rings ums Leben verherrlicht habt,
Soll mutlos kehren?

Vater Bromius!
Du bist Genius,
Jahrhunderts Genius,
Bist, was innre Glut
Pindarn war,
Was der Welt
Phöbus Apoll ist.

Weh! Weh! Innre Wärme,
Seelenwärme,
Mittelpunkt!
Glüh' entgegen
Phöb' Apollen;
Kalt wird sonst
Sein Fürstenblick
Über dich vorübergleiten,
Neidgetroffen
Auf der Zeder Kraft verweilen,
Die zu grünen
Sein nicht harrt.

You are pure, like the heart of the waters,
You are pure, like the marrow of earth,
You hover around me, and I hover
Over water, over earth,
Like the gods.

*

Shall he find his way home,
The small, the dark, the fiery peasant,
Shall he find his way home, expecting
Only your gifts, Father Bromius,
And bright-glowing, warmth-giving fire?
Shall he return hopeful?
And I whom you attended,
Muses and Graces in numbers,
I for whom everything waits
That you, Muses and Graces,
Have glorified round about life—
Blissfulness crowning my brow—,
Shall I return hopeless?

Father Bromius!
You are Genius,
The century's Genius,
Are what inner glow
To Pindar was,
What to the world
Is Phoebus Apollo.

Wo! Wo! Inner warmth,
Warmth of the soul,
The center!
Send a glow
Toward Phoebus Apollo,
Else his lordly eye
Will glide cold
Over your head and past you,
Struck by envy
And rest on the sturdy cedar,
Green and alive
Without his help.

Warum nennt mein Lied dich zuletzt?
Dich, von dem es begann,
Dich, in dem es endet,
Dich, aus dem es quillt,
Jupiter Pluvius!
Dich, dich strömt mein Lied,
Und kastalischer Quell
Rinnt ein Nebenbach,
Rinnet Müssigen,
Sterblich Glücklichen
Abseits von dir,
Der du mich fassend deckst,
Jupiter Pluvius!

Nicht am Ulmenbaum
Hast du ihn besucht,
Mit dem Taubenpaar
In dem zärtlichen Arm,
Mit der freundlichen Ros' umkränzt,
Tändelnden ihn, blumenglücklichen
Anakreon,
Sturmatmende Gottheit!

Nicht im Pappelwald
An des Sybaris Strand,
An des Gebirgs
Sonnebeglänzter Stirn nicht
Fasstest du ihn,
Den Bienen singenden
Honig lallenden,
Freundlich winkenden
Theokrit.

Wenn die Räder rasselten,
Rad an Rad ums Ziel weg,
Hoch flog
Siegdurchglühter
Jünglinge Peitschenknall,
Und sich Staub wälzt',
Wie vom Gebirg herab
Kieselwetter ins Tal,
Glühte deine Seel' Gefahren, Pindar,
Mut.—Glühte?—

Why does my song name you the last
You from whom it began,
You in whom it will end,
You from whom it springs,
Jupiter Pluvius!
You, you are showered by my song,
And this Castalian fount
Runs as a brooklet,
Runs for the idle,
Mortal happy ones,
Off to your side,
You who grasp me and cover me,
Jupiter Pluvius!

Not at the elm tree,
Jove, did you seek him
With the pair of doves
In his tender arm,
And wreathed with the friendly rose—
That dallying poet happy with flowers,
Anacreon,
You, storm-breathing godhead!

Not in the poplar wood,
Not at the Sybarites' shore,
At the mountains'
Sun-illumined brow not
Did you seize him,
That poet singing of bees,
That mellifluous
Friendly beckoning
Theocritus.

When the wheels were rattling,
Wheel on wheel, round, past the goal,
And high flew
The snap of the whip
Of youths flushed with victory,
And dust-clouds rolled,
As down from the mountain
Hailstones crash to the valley,
Your soul glowed with courage, o Pindar,
In face of danger. Glowed?

Armes Herz!
Dort auf dem Hügel,
Himmlische Macht!
Nur so viel Glut:
Dort meine Hütte,
Dorthin zu waten!

6. MAHOMETS GESANG

Seht den Felsenquell,
Freudehell,
Wie ein Sternenblick!
Über Wolken
Nährten seine Jugend
Gute Geister
Zwischen Klippen im Gebüsch.

Jünglingfrisch
Tanzt er aus der Wolke
Auf die Marmorfelsen nieder,
Jauchzet wieder
Nach dem Himmel.

Durch die Gipfelgänge
Jagt er bunten Kieseln nach,
Und mit frühem Führertritt
Reisst er seine Bruderquellen
Mit sich fort.

Drunten werden in dem Tal
Unter seinem Fusstritt Blumen,
Und die Wiese
Lebt von seinem Hauch.

Doch ihn hält kein Schattental,
Keine Blumen,
Die ihm seine Knie' umschlingen,
Ihm mit Liebesaugen schmeicheln:
Nach der Ebne dringt sein Lauf,
Schlangenwandelnd.

Bäche schmiegen
Sich gesellig an. Nun tritt er
In die Ebne silberprangend,

Poor heart!
There on the hilltop,
Heavenly power!
Only so much glow
Thither to wade
Where stands my hut.

6. MAHOMET'S SONG

See the rock-born stream
Brightly gleam,
Like the stars that shine!
Kindly spirits
Nourished him while youthful
Over cloudbanks
Mid the crags in undergrowth.

Young and fresh
From a cloud he dances
Down upon the cliffs of marble,
Then toward heaven
Leaps exulting.

Through the channeled summits
He pursues the colored stones,
With a youthful leader's pace
Sweeps along his brother-freshets
In his course.

In the valley down below,
Underfoot the flowers flourish,
And the meadow
Lives but from his breath.

Him no shadowed vale can hold,
Nor can flowers,
Which around his knees are twining,
Flattering him with eyes of passion.
At the plain his course is aimed,
Serpent-winding.

Brooks come nestling
As companions. Now he enters
On the plain in silvery splendor,

Und die Ebne prangt mit ihm,
Und die Flüsse von der Ebne
Und die Bäche von den Bergen
Jauchzen ihm und rufen: Bruder!
Bruder, nimm die Brüder mit,
Mit zu deinem alten Vater,
Zu dem ew'gen Ozean,
Der mit ausgespannten Armen
Unser wartet,
Die sich, ach! vergebens öffnen,
Seine Sehnenden zu fassen:
Denn uns frisst in öder Wüste
Gier'ger Sand, die Sonne droben
Saugt an unserm Blut, ein Hügel
Hemmet uns zum Teiche! Bruder,
Nimm die Brüder von der Ebne,
Nimm die Brüder von den Bergen
Mit, zu deinem Vater mit!

Kommt ihr alle!—
Und nun schwillt er
Herrlicher: ein ganz Geschlechte
Trägt den Fürsten hoch empor!
Und im rollenden Triumphe
Gibt er Ländern Namen, Städte
Werden unter seinem Fuss.

Unaufhaltsam rauscht er weiter,
Lässt der Türme Flammengipfel,
Marmorhäuser, eine Schöpfung
Seiner Fülle, hinter sich.

Zedernhäuser trägt der Atlas
Auf den Riesenschultern; sausend
Wehen über seinem Haupte
Tausend Flaggen durch die Lüfte,
Zeugen seiner Herrlichkeit.

Und so trägt er seine Brüder,
Seine Schätze, seine Kinder
Dem erwartenden Erzeuger
Freudebrausend an das Herz.

And with him the plain is bright,
And the rivers from the plainland,
And the brooklets from the hilltops
Greet him and exult: Our brother!
Brother, take your brethren too,
Come and join your aged Father,
In the Ocean's timelessness,
Who with arms outstretched to greet us
Waits our coming,
Arms that, ah, in vain are open
To embrace his yearning children.
For the thirsty sand consumes us
In the desert waste; the sunshine
Sucks our blood, and hills around us
Make of us a pond! O brother,
Take your brethren from the plainland,
Take your brethren from the hilltops,
Take them to your Father's arms!

Come, come all, then!
Now he swells up
Lordlier: a generation
Bears the princely stream on high!
And in triumph onward rolling,
He gives names to countries; cities
Spring up where he flows along.

Unrestrained he rushes onward,
Leaves the towers' flaming summits,
Marble houses, a creation
Of his fulness, far behind.

Cedar ships this Atlas poises
On his giant-shoulders; swishing
Countless banners wave and flutter
Far above his head on breezes,
Bearing witness to his might.

And 'tis thus he bears his brothers,
All his treasures, all his children,
To his waiting Maker's bosom,
To the Ocean roaring joy.

7. HARZREISE IM WINTER

Dem Geier gleich,
Der auf schweren Morgenwolken
Mit sanftem Fittich ruhend
Nach Beute schaut,
Schwebe mein Lied.

Denn ein Gott hat
Jedem seine Bahn
Vorgezeichnet,
Die der Glückliche
Rasch zum freudigen
Ziele rennt:
Wem aber Unglück
Das Herz zusammenzog,
Er sträubt vergebens
Sich gegen die Schranken
Des ehernen Fadens,
Den die doch bittre Schere
Nur einmal löst.

In Dickichts-Schauer
Drängt sich das rauhe Wild,
Und mit den Sperlingen
Haben längst die Reichen
In ihre Sümpfe sich gesenkt.

Leicht ists folgen dem Wagen,
Den Fortuna führt,
Wie der gemächliche Tross
Auf gebesserten Wegen
Hinter des Fürsten Einzug.

Aber abseits wer ists?
Ins Gebüsch verliert sich sein Pfad,
Hinter ihm schlagen
Die Sträuche zusammen,
Das Gras steht wieder auf,
Die Öde verschlingt ihn.

Ach, wer heilet die Schmerzen
Dess, dem Balsam zu Gift ward?
Der sich Menschenhass

7. WINTER JOURNEY TO THE HARZ MOUNTAINS

    As a vulture would,
That on heavy clouds of morning
With gentle wing reposing,
Seeks for his prey—
Hover, my song.

    For a God has
Prescribed to everyone
His destined course,
Which the happy man
Pursues swiftly
To his joyous goal:
He whose heart fate has
Tightly constricted,
Combats but vainly
All of the barriers
The brazen thread offers,
But which the rasping shears
Cuts once for all.

    'Mid gloomy thickets
Wild game is pressing on,
And with the sparrows' flock
Long have the wealthy
Settled themselves in their marshes.

    'Tis easy to follow the wheels
That Fortune steers,
Like the slow-moving train
On well-mended highways
That follows the prince.

    But who's that to one side?
In the thicket lost is his trail,
Behind him the bushes
Are closing together,
The grass rises again,
The wilderness gulfs him.

    Ah, who'll heal his afflictions
Whom balsam has poisoned,
Who from love's fulness

Aus der Fülle der Liebe trank?
Erst verachtet, nun ein Verächter,
Zehrt er heimlich auf
Seinen eignen Wert
In ungnügender Selbstsucht.

Ist auf deinem Psalter,
Vater der Liebe, ein Ton
Seinem Ohre vernehmlich,
So erquicke sein Herz!
Öffne den umwölkten Blick
Über die tausend Quellen
Neben dem Durstenden
In der Wüste.

Der du der Freuden viel schaffst,
Jedem ein überfliessend Mass,
Segne die Brüder der Jagd
Auf der Fährte des Wilds
Mit jugendlichem Übermut
Fröhlicher Mordsucht,
Späte Rächer des Unbills,
Dem schon Jahre vergeblich
Wehrt mit Knütteln der Bauer.

Aber den Einsamen hüll
In deine Goldwolken!
Umgib mit Wintergrün,
Bis die Rose wieder heranreift,
Die feuchten Haare,
O Liebe, deines Dichters!

Mit der dämmernden Fackel
Leuchtest du ihm
Durch die Furten bei Nacht,
Über grundlose Wege
Auf öden Gefilden;
Mit dem tausendfarbigen Morgen
Lachst du ins Herz ihm;
Mit dem beizenden Sturm
Trägst du ihn hoch empor;
Winterstürme stürzen vom Felsen
In seine Psalmen,

Quaffed hatred of mankind?
First despised, and now a despiser,
He in secret consumes
His very own worth
In self-love that's restive.

If there be on thy psalter,
Father of love, but one note
That by his ear can be heard,
O then quicken his heart!
Open his cloud-enveloped eyes
Over the thousand well-springs
Close by the thirsty man
In the desert.

Father, creating much joy,
For each a measure o'erbrimming,
Bless the sons of the chase
On the track of the game
With the abandon of youth,
Happy in killing—
Late in avenging injustice
Resisted by peasants
Vainly for years with their clubs.

But the lonely man, veil him
In Thy clouds of gold!
Surround with wintergreen
(Till the rose may blossom again),
The locks so humid,
O, Love, of Thy singer!

With Thy torch and its glimmer
Thou givest him light
Through the fords of the night,
Over bottomless spaces
On plains of the desert,
With the thousand hues of the morning
Exulting his heart;
With the fierce-biting storm
Bearest him proudly aloft.
Wintery torrents rush from the cliffs
And blend with his psalms,

Und Altar des lieblichsten Danks
Wird ihm des gefürchteten Gipfels
Schneebehangner Scheitel,
Den mit Geisterreihen
Kränzten ahnende Völker.

Du stehst mit unerforschtem Busen
Geheimnisvoll offenbar
Über der erstaunten Welt
Und schaust aus Wolken
Auf ihre Reiche und Herrlichkeit,
Die du aus den Adern deiner Brüder
Neben dir wässerst.

And an altar of grateful delight
He finds on the much-dreaded mountain's
Snow-begirded summit
Which foreboding peoples
Have crowned with spirit-dances.

   Thou standest with inscrutable breast,
Mysteriously revealed
Over the wondering world
And peerest from clouds
Upon its realms and its majesty
Which Thou from the veins of Thy brethren
Near Thee dost water.

CHAPTER II. FROM "WILHELM MEISTER"

1. MIGNON 1.

Heiss mich nicht reden, heiss mich schweigen,
Denn mein Geheimnis ist mir Pflicht;
Ich möchte dir mein ganzes Innre zeigen,
Allein das Schicksal will es nicht.

Zur rechten Zeit vertreibt der Sonne Lauf
Die finstre Nacht, und sie muss sich erhellen;
Der harte Fels schliesst seinen Busen auf,
Missgönnt der Erde nicht die tiefverborgnen Quellen.

Ein jeder sucht im Arm des Freundes Ruh,
Dort kann die Brust in Klagen sich ergiessen;
Allein ein Schwur drückt mir die Lippen zu,
Und nur ein Gott vermag sie aufzuschliessen.

2. MIGNON 2.

So lasst mich scheinen, bis ich werde,
Zieht mir das weisse Kleid nicht aus!
Ich eile von der schönen Erde
Hinab in jenes feste Haus.

Dort ruh' ich eine kleine Stille,
Dann öffnet sich der frische Blick;
Ich lasse dann die reine Hülle,
Den Gürtel und den Kranz zurück.

Und jene himmlischen Gestalten,
Sie fragen nicht nach Mann und Weib,
Und keine Kleider, keine Falten
Umgeben den verklärten Leib.

Zwar lebt' ich ohne Sorg' und Mühe,
Doch fühlt' ich tiefen Schmerz genung;
Vor Kummer altert' ich zu frühe—
Macht mich auf ewig wieder jung!

3. PHILINE

Singet nicht in Trauertönen
Von der Einsamkeit der Nacht:
Nein, sie ist, o holde Schönen,
Zur Geselligkeit gemacht.

From "Wilhelm Meister"

1. MIGNON 1.

Bid me not speak, silence behooves me!
My secret is a pledge to me.
I'd show you all the hidden grief that moves me,
But fate has willed it differently.

When time is ripe, the dark and gloomy night
Will fade before the sun as light progresses,
The hard cliff open up its bosom wide,
Begrudging not the earth its springs in deep recesses.

In some dear friend's embrace we all seek rest,
There can the heart pour woes out and reveal them.
An oath of silence on my lips is pressed,
Only a god has power to unseal them.

2. MIGNON 2.

So let me seem until I'm chastened
In heaven; spare my dress of white!
Till I from this fair earth have hastened
Into that house so firm and tight.

A little respite there I'll find me,
Until there looms a brighter heath.
The spotless shroud I'll leave behind me
And shed the girdle and the wreath.

Those forms beyond the heavenly portals
Ask not if man or wife we be,
Nor will the robes or folds of mortals,
When I'm transfigured, cover me.

No care nor trouble did I borrow,
But grief I felt, a bounteous store.
I aged too soon in all my sorrow—
O make me ever young once more!

5. PHILINE

Sing no songs in mourning sadness
Of the solitude of night.
Night, fair maids, is meant for gladness
And for sociable delight.

Wie das Weib dem Mann gegeben
Als die schönste Hälfte war,
Ist die Nacht das halbe Leben,
Und die schönste Hälfte zwar.

Könnt ihr euch des Tages freuen,
Der nur Freuden unterbricht?
Er ist gut, sich zu zerstreuen,
Zu was anderm taugt er nicht.

Aber wenn in nächt'ger Stunde
Süsser Lampe Dämmrung fliesst
Und vom Mund zum nahen Munde
Scherz und Liebe sich ergiesst;

Wenn der rasche lose Knabe,
Der sonst wild und feurig eilt,
Oft bei einer kleinen Gabe
Unter leichten Spielen weilt;

Wenn die Nachtigall Verliebten
Liebevoll ein Liedchen singt,
Das Gefangnen und Betrübten
Nur wie Ach und Wehe klingt:

Mit wie leichtem Herzensregen
Horchet ihr der Glocke nicht,
Die mit zwölf bedächt'gen Schlägen
Ruh und Sicherheit verspricht!

Darum an dem langen Tage
Merke dir es, liebe Brust:
Jeder Tag hat seine Plage,
Und die Nacht hat ihre Lust.

From "Wilhelm Meister"

Just as man is given a wife
And she's the fairest half to see,
So the night is half of life
And ah! the best half truthfully.

Can the daytime ever please you
When it thwarts your joyful mood?
With diversion it can tease you,
And it serves no other good.

But when in nocturnal hours
Fitful-dim sweet lamplight glows,
And when love or jesting flowers,
As from mouth to mouth it goes;

When that boy, rash wayward rover,
Wont to be impetuous,
Lingers, over toys to hover,
Where he joins in play with us;

When the nightingale is singing
Love songs meant for lovers' cheer,
Which like sighs and wails keep ringing
In the mournful captive's ear:

How your heart throbs soft with feeling
When you hear the steeple chime
That with twelvefold solemn pealing
Tolls the safely restful time!

So in days whose length seems double
Mark it, heart, attentively:
Every day begets its trouble,
And the night its ecstasy.

CHAPTER III. ITALY

1. RÖMISCHE ELEGIE X

Alexander und Cäsar und Heinrich und Friedrich, die Grossen,
  Gäben die Hälfte mir gern ihres erworbenen Ruhms,
Könnt ich auf Eine Nacht dies Lager jedem vergönnen;
  Aber die armen, sie hält strenge des Orkus Gewalt.
Freue dich also, Lebendger, der lieberwärmeten Stätte,
  Ehe den fliehenden Fuss schauerlich Lethe dir netzt.

2. RÖMISCHE ELEGIE XVII

Manche Töne sind mir Verdruss, doch bleibet am meisten
  Hundegebell mir verhasst; kläffend zerreisst es mein Ohr.
Einen Hund nur hör' ich sehr oft mit frohem Behagen
  Bellend kläffen, den Hund, den sich der Nachbar erzog.
Denn er bellte mir einst mein Mädchen an, da sie sich heimlich
  Zu mir stahl, und verriet unser Geheimnis beinah.
Jetzo, hör' ich ihn bellen, so denk' ich nur immer: sie kommt wohl!
  Oder ich denke der Zeit, da die Erwartete kam.

3. EPIGRAMME. VENEDIG. 5.

In der Gondel lag ich gestreckt und fuhr durch die Schiffe,
  Die in dem grossen Kanal, viele befrachtete, stehn.
Mancherlei Ware findest du da für manches Bedürfnis,
  Weizen, Wein und Gemüs, Scheite, wie leichtes Gesträuch.
Pfeilschnell drangen wir durch; da traf ein verlorener Lorbeer
  Derb mir die Wangen. Ich rief: Daphne, verletzest du mich?
Lohn erwartet ich eher! Die Nymphe lispelte lächelnd:
  Dichter sündgen nicht schwer. Leicht ist die Strafe. Nur zu!

4. EPIGRAMME. VENEDIG. 8.

Diese Gondel vergleich' ich der sanft einschaukelnden Wiege,
  Und das Kästchen darauf scheint ein geräumiger Sarg.
Recht so! Zwischen der Wieg' und dem Sarg wir schwanken und schweben
  Auf dem grossen Kanal sorglos durch's Leben dahin.

ITALY

1. ROMAN ELEGY X

Alexander and Caesar and Henry and Frederick, the mighty,
  Gladly would give up to me half of the glory they earned,
Could I grant each of the four one night on the couch where
    I'm lying;
  But they, pitiful men, sternly by Orcus are held.
Therefore rejoice while you live, that yours is a love-lighted
    homestead,
  Ere River Lethe with dread moistens your fugitive foot.

2. ROMAN ELEGY XVII

Many noises annoy me, but most of all noises the piercing
  Bark of a dog; his shrill yelping tears at my ear.
One dog only I hear that often causes me pleasure,
  Barking loudly—the dog kept by my neighbor next door.
Once he barked at my girl when she was stealthily nearing,
  Bent on a visit to me, almost exposing our tryst.
Now when I hear him barking, I always think: She is coming,
  Or I think of the time when, as expected, she came.

3. VENETIAN EPIGRAM 5

Prone in the gondola lying I glided by where the vessels
  Lie in the Grand Canal, heavily freighted and moored.
Manifold wares you will find for manifold uses intended,
  Wheat, many greens and wine, logs and shrubs weighing light.
Quick as an arrow we passed, when at once a wildering laurel
  Whipped at my cheek. I cried: "Daphne, you're injuring me?
Sooner I hoped for reward!" With a smile the nymph murmured
    her answer:
  "Poets' sins are not great. Gentle the punishment. Go!"

4. VENETIAN EPIGRAM 8

I would compare this gondola's form to a soft-rocking cradle,
  While the chest on its deck seems a huge coffin to me.
Right, between cradle and coffin we totter and waver forever
  On the mighty canal, carefree our lifetime is spent.

5. EPIGRAMME. VENEDIG. 10.

Warum treibt sich das Volk so, und schreit? Es will sich ernähren,
  Kinder zeugen, und die nähren, so gut es vermag.
Merke dir, Reisender, das und tue zu Hause desgleichen!
  Weiter bringt es kein Mensch, stell er sich, wie er auch will.

6. EPIGRAMME. VENEDIG. 96.

Glänzen sah ich das Meer, und blinken die liebliche Welle,
  Frisch mit günstigem Wind zogen die Segel dahin.
Keine Sehnsucht fühlte mein Herz; es wendete rückwärts,
  Nach dem Schnee des Gebirgs, bald sich der schmachtende Blick.
Südwärts liegen der Schätze wie viel. Doch einer im Norden
  Zieht, ein grosser Magnet, unwiderstehlich zurück.

5. VENETIAN EPIGRAM 10

Why are the people stirring and shouting? For food they are
 seeking,
Children they would beget, feed them as well as they can.
Traveller, mark this well, and when you are home, do you
 likewise!
More can no mortal achieve, try with what effort he will.

6. VENETIAN EPIGRAM 96

Gleaming I saw the ocean, and smiling the beautiful billow,
 Freshly a favoring wind, filling the sails, drove us on.
Free was my heart from yearning, yet soon my eyes in their ardor
 Turned to cast glances behind, seeking the snow-covered hills.
Southward treasures are lying, how many! But one in the north-
 land,
 Like a huge magnet, with force draws me resistlessly back.

CHAPTER IV. POEMS OF MATURITY

1. ALEXIS UND DORA

Ach! unaufhaltsam strebet das Schiff mit jedem Momente
  Durch die schäumende Flut weiter und weiter hinaus!
Langhin furcht sich die Gleise des Kiels, worin die Delphine
  Springend folgen, als flöh' ihnen die Beute davon.
Alles deutet auf glückliche Fahrt: der ruhige Bootsmann
  Ruckt am Segel gelind, das sich für alle bemüht;
Vorwärts dringt der Schiffenden Geist, wie Flaggen und Wimpel.
Einer nur steht rückwärts traurig gewendet am Mast,
Sieht die Berge schon blau, die scheidenden, sieht in das Meer sie
  Niedersinken, es sinkt jegliche Freude vor ihm.
Auch dir ist es verschwunden, das Schiff, das deinen Alexis,
  Dir, o Dora, den Freund, ach! dir den Bräutigam raubt.
Auch du blickest vergebens nach mir. Noch schlagen die Herzen
  Für einander, doch ach! nun an einander nicht mehr.
Einziger Augenblick, in welchem ich lebte! du wiegest
  Alle Tage, die sonst kalt mir verschwindenden, auf.
Ach! nur im Augenblick, im letzten, stieg mir ein Leben
  Unvermutet in dir, wie von den Göttern, herab.
Nur umsonst verklärst du mit deinem Lichte den Äther,
  Dein alleuchtender Tag, Phöbus, mir ist er verhasst.
In mich selber kehr' ich zurück: da will ich im stillen
  Wiederholen die Zeit, als sie mir täglich erschien.
War es möglich, die Schönheit zu sehn und nicht zu empfinden?
  Wirkte der himmlische Reiz nicht auf dein stumpfes Gemüt?
Klage dich, Armer, nicht an!—So legt der Dichter ein Rätsel,
  Künstlich mit Worten verschränkt, oft der Versammlung ins Ohr:
Jeden freuet die seltne, der zierlichen Bilder Verknüpfung,
  Aber noch fehlt das Wort, das die Bedeutung verwahrt;
Ist es endlich entdeckt, dann heitert sich jedes Gemüt auf
  Und erblickt im Gedicht doppelt erfreulichen Sinn.
Ach, warum so spät, o Amor, nahmst du die Binde,
  Die du ums Aug' mir geknüpft, nahmst sie zu spät mir hinweg!
Lange schon harrte befrachtet das Schiff auf günstige Lüfte;
  Endlich strebte der Wind glücklich vom Ufer ins Meer.
Leere Zeiten der Jugend! und leere Träume der Zukunft!

1. ALEXIS AND DORA

Ah, with progress unchecked each moment the vessel advances,
 Cleaving the foam-covered flood, onward and outward it glides!
Long is the wake plowed up by the keel where dolphins are leaping,
 Eager to follow its course, fearing the booty's escape.
All presages a prosperous voyage; the sailor with calmness
 Gently pulls at the sail, this does service for all.
Forward presses each seafarer's heart, like banners and streamers.
 Only one stands aft, sadly facing the mast,
Sees the mountains of blue recede and sink in the ocean,
 And as they disappear, joy sinks too in his breast.
Vanished from you, o Dora, is now the vessel that robs you,
 Taking Alexis, your friend, ah, your betrothed from your arms.
Your eyes too follow me in vain, but our hearts are still throbbing
 For each other yet, ah, far from each other they throb.
Oh, that one rare moment of life that richly requited
 All my days that had fled cold and meaningless too.
Ah, in that moment alone, the last one, life was allowed me
 Through you, as by the gods, though I suspected it not.
Phoebus, in vain with your rays you bathe the ether in glory!
 Your all-brightening day, hateful I find it to be.
Into my inmost self I retreat, and there, in the silence,
 Strive to live over the time when with each day *she* appeared.
Could I see beauty like this, and seeing it, still never feel it?
 Could not those heavenly charms work on my spirit so dull?
Blame not yourself, you wretch!—A poet is fond of proposing
 Riddles like this to the throng, skilfully woven in words.
Everyone likes the strange commingling of delicate symbols,
 Still we are lacking the word wherein is hidden the sense.
When at last it is found, each reader's spirit is gladdened,
 And in the poem he sees meaning of double delight.
Why, o Cupid, so late did you free my sight of the bondage
 Which you had placed on my eyes,—why was it lifted so late?
Long had the vessel, all laden, been waiting for favoring breezes,
 Till the zephyrs at last blew from the land o'er the sea.
Empty times of youth and empty dreams of the future!

Ihr verschwindet, es bleibt einzig die Stunde mir nur.
Ja, sie bleibt, es bleibt mir das Glück! ich halte dich, Dora!
   Und die Hoffnung zeigt, Dora, dein Bild mir allein.
Öfter sah ich zum Tempel dich gehn, geschmückt und gesittet,
   Und das Mütterchen ging feierlich neben dir her.
Eilig warst du und frisch, zu Markte die Früchte zu tragen,
   Und vom Brunnen, wie kühn! wiegte dein Haupt das Gefäss.
Da erschien dein Hals, erschien dein Nacken vor allen,
   Und vor allen erschien deiner Bewegungen Mass.
Oftmals hab' ich gesorgt, es möchte der Krug dir entstürzen,
   Doch er hielt sich stet auf dem geringelten Tuch.
Schöne Nachbarin, ja, so war ich gewohnt dich zu sehen,
   Wie man die Sterne sieht, wie man den Mond sich beschaut,
Sich an ihnen erfreut, und innen im ruhigen Busen
   Nicht der entfernteste Wunsch, sie zu besitzen, sich regt.
Jahre, so gingt ihr dahin! Nur zwanzig Schritte getrennet
   Waren die Häuser, und nie hab' ich die Schwelle berührt.
Und nun trennt uns die grässliche Flut! Du lügst nur den Himmel,
   Welle! dein herrliches Blau ist mir die Farbe der Nacht.
Alles rührte sich schon; da kam ein Knabe gelaufen
   An mein väterlich Haus, rief mich zum Strande hinab:
Schon erhebt sich das Segel, es flattert im Winde, so sprach er,
   Und gelichtet, mit Kraft, trennt sich der Anker vom Sand;
Komm, Alexis, o komm! Da drückte der wackere Vater
   Würdig die segnende Hand mir auf das lockige Haupt;
Sorglich reichte die Mutter ein nachbereitetes Bündel:
   Glücklich kehre zurück! riefen sie, glücklich und reich!
Und so sprang ich hinweg, das Bündelchen unter dem Arme,
   An der Mauer hinab, fand an der Türe dich stehn
Deines Gartens. Du lächeltest mir und sagtest: Alexis!
   Sind die Lärmenden dort deine Gesellen der Fahrt?
Fremde Küsten besuchest du nun, und köstliche Waren
   Handelst du ein, und Schmuck reichen Matronen der Stadt.
Aber bringe mir auch ein leichtes Kettchen; ich will es
   Dankbar zahlen: so oft hab' ich die Zierde gewünscht!
Stehen war ich geblieben und fragte, nach Weise des Kaufmanns,

You are gone; there remains only a moment for me.
Yes, it remains, my joy still remains! I hold you, my Dora,
   And your image alone, Dora, by hope is revealed.
Often I saw you go, with modesty decked, to the temple,
   While the mother you love solemnly went by your side.
Eager and nimble you were, in bearing your fruit to the market,
   Boldly the vase from the well poised you held on your head.
Then I could see your neck, could see your shoulders, the fairest,
   Then, above all, the grace marking each movement you made.
Often I feared that the pitcher you bore was in danger of falling,
   Still it remained there firm over the fold of the cloth.
So, fair neighbor, yes so, I often was wont to observe you,
   As a man studies the stars, as he may gaze on the moon,
Happy over the sight, yet never within his calm bosom
   Feeling remotest desire ever to call them his own.
Years thus passed on their way! Although our houses were only
   Twenty paces apart, never I darkened your door.
Now the terrible flood must part us! You're aping the heavens,
   Billow! Your beautiful blue seems to me darkness of night.
All were already astir, when a boy to the house of my father
   Hurried his step and exclaimed: "Come at full speed to the shore,
Come, they are hoisting the sail, and see, in the wind it is fluttering.
   Stoutly the anchor they weigh, heaving it up from the sand.
Come, Alexis, o come."—With a dignified mien my good father,
   Blessing me, pressed his hand down on my curly-locked head,
While my mother thoughtfully gave me a newly made bundle:
   "Happily may you return, happy and wealthy!" they cried.
Then I hastened away, and under my arm held the bundle,
   Running along by the wall. There you were standing not far
By your garden gate, when you smiled and whispered: "Alexis!
   Tell me, that boisterous crew, are they your comrades to be?
Foreign coasts you will visit, and precious wares you will purchase,
   Jewels for matrons of wealth dwelling there in the town,
Bring me also, I beg you, a light chain; gladly I'll pay you.
   Often I've longed to possess some such adornment as that."
There I had stopped and asked, as merchants would do, with preciseness,

Erst nach Form und Gewicht deiner Bestellung genau.
Gar bescheiden erwogst du den Preis! da blickt' ich indessen
　Nach dem Halse, des Schmucks unserer Königin wert.
Heftiger tönte vom Schiff das Geschrei; da sagtest du freundlich:
　Nimm aus dem Garten noch einige Früchte mit dir!
Nimm die reifsten Orangen, die weissen Feigen; das Meer bringt
　Keine Früchte, sie bringt jegliches Land nicht hervor.
Und so trat ich herein. Du brachst nun die Früchte geschäftig,
　Und die goldene Last zog das geschürzte Gewand.
Öfters bat ich: es sei nun genug! und immer noch eine
　Schönere Frucht fiel dir, leise berührt, in die Hand.
Endlich kamst du zur Laube hinan; da fand sich ein Körbchen,
　Und die Myrte bog blühend sich über uns hin.
Schweigend begannest du nun geschickt die Früchte zu ordnen:
　Erst die Orange, die schwer ruht, als ein goldener Ball,
Dann die weichliche Feige, die jeder Druck schon entstellet;
　Und mit Myrte bedeckt ward und geziert das Geschenk.
Aber ich hob es nicht auf; ich stand. Wir sahen einander
　In die Augen, und mir ward vor dem Auge so trüb.
Deinen Busen fühlt' ich an meinem! Den herrlichen Nacken,
　Ihn umschlang nun mein Arm, tausendmal küsst' ich den Hals.
Mir sank über die Schulter dein Haupt: nun knüpften auch deine
　Lieblichen Arme das Band um den Beglückten herum.
Amors Hände fühlt' ich: er drückt' uns gewaltig zusammen,
　Und aus heiterer Luft donnert' es dreimal. Da floss
Häufig die Träne vom Aug' mir herab, du weintest, ich weinte,
　Und vor Jammer und Glück schien uns die Welt zu vergehn.
Immer heftiger rief es am Strand; da wollten die Füsse
　Mich nicht tragen, ich rief: Dora! und bist du nicht mein?
Ewig! sagtest du leise. Da schienen unsere Tränen,
　Wie durch göttliche Luft, leise vom Auge gehaucht.
Näher rief es: Alexis! Da blickte der suchende Knabe
　Durch die Türe herein. Wie er das Körbchen empfing!
Wie er mich trieb! Wie ich dir die Hand noch drückte!—Zu
　Schiffe

After the form and the weight which your necklace should have.
Modest indeed was the price that you named: I meanwhile was gazing
On your neck which deserved ornaments worn by our queen.
Louder now rose the cry from the ship; then kindly your words came:
"Take for your journey some fruit out of the garden, my friend!
Take the ripest oranges, take the white figs, for the ocean
Bears no fruit, and indeed, neither does many a land."
So I entered the garden. You plucked the fruit, never pausing,
And the burden of gold lay in the fold of your dress.
Often I begged you: Enough! But fairer fruit was still falling
Into your hand as I spoke, gently obeying your touch.
Finally then you came to the arbor; you found there a basket,
Where the myrtle bowed, blooming over our heads.
Then you began to arrange the fruit with skill and in silence:
First the orange, which lay heavy as though 'twere of gold,
Then the susceptible fig, by the gentlest pressure disfigured,
And with myrtle the gift soon was covered and decked.
But I left it untouched. I stood. We looked at each other
Eye to eye, my sight seemed to me dim and obscured.
Soon I felt your bosom on mine! My arm ere I knew it
Clasped your beautiful form, kisses showered your neck.
On my shoulder rested your head, fair arms then embraced me,
Forming a circle of love, spelling rapture for me.
Cupid's hands I felt: he pressed us together with vigor,
And from a sky that was clear thrice did it thunder. Then tears
Streamed from my eyes in a torrent, you wept, I wept, both were weeping,
And in our sorrow and bliss even our world seemed to die.
Louder and louder they called from the shore; my feet would no longer
Carry my weight, and I cried: "Dora, and are you not mine?"
"Yours forever!" you whispered. And then the tears we were shedding
Gently were brushed from our eyes, as by the breath of a god.
Nearer we heard the cry: "Alexis!" The boy who had sought me
Suddenly peered through the gate. How he took basket in hand!
How he urged me away! How I pressed your hand! If you ask me

Wie ich gekommen? Ich weiss, dass ich ein Trunkener schien.
Und so hielten mich auch die Gesellen, schonten den Kranken;
  Und schon deckte der Hauch trüber Entfernung die Stadt.
Ewig! Dora, lispeltest du; mir schallt es im Ohre
  Mit dem Donner des Zeus! Stand sie doch neben dem Thron,
Seine Tochter, die Göttin der Liebe, die Grazien standen
  Ihr zur Seiten! Er ist götterbekräftigt, der Bund!
O, so eile denn, Schiff, mit allen günstigen Winden!
  Strebe, mächtiger Kiel, trenne die schäumende Flut!
Bringe dem fremden Hafen mich zu, damit mir der Goldschmied
  In der Werkstatt gleich ordne das himmlische Pfand.
Wahrlich! Zur Kette soll das Kettchen werden, o Dora!
  Neunmal umgebe sie dir, locker gewunden, den Hals!
Ferner schaff' ich noch Schmuck, den mannigfaltigsten: goldne
  Spangen sollen dir auch reichlich verzieren die Hand.
Da wetteifre Rubin und Smaragd, der liebliche Saphir
  Stelle dem Hyazinth sich gegenüber, und Gold
Halte das Edelgestein in schöner Verbindung zusammen.
  O, wie den Bräutigam freut, einzig zu schmücken die Braut!
Seh' ich Perlen, so denk' ich an dich; bei jeglichem Ringe
  Kommt mir der länglichen Hand schönes Gebild' in den Sinn.
Tauschen will ich und kaufen; du sollst das Schönste von allem
  Wählen; ich widmete gern alle die Ladung nur dir.
Doch nicht Schmuck und Juwelen allein verschafft dein Geliebter:
  Was ein häusliches Weib freuet, das bringt er dir auch.
Feine wollene Decken mit Purpursäumen, ein Lager
  Zu bereiten, das uns traulich und weichlich empfängt;
Köstlicher Leinwand Stücke. Du sitzest und nähest und kleidest
  Mich und dich und auch wohl noch ein drittes darein.
Bilder der Hoffnung, täuschet mein Herz! O, mässiget, Götter,
  Diesen gewaltigen Brand, der mir den Busen durchtobt!
Aber auch sie verlang' ich zurück, die schmerzliche Freude,
  Wenn die Sorge sich kalt, grässlich gelassen, mir naht.
Nicht der Erinnyen Fackel, das Bellen der höllischen Hunde
  Schreckt den Verbrecher so in der Verzweiflung Gefild,
Als das gelassne Gespenst mich schreckt, das die Schöne von fern mir
  Zeiget: die Türe steht wirklich des Gartens noch auf!
Und ein anderer kommt! Für ihn auch fallen die Früchte!
  Und die Feige gewährt stärkenden Honig auch ihm!
Lockt sie auch ihn nach der Laube? und folgt er? O, macht mich,
  ihr Götter,

How I reached the ship, drunken I seemed, well I know.
  Drunken my shipmates believed me, and so had pity upon me;
    Distance gloomily cast haze on the vanishing town.
"Yours forever!" Dora, you murmured; it rings in my senses
  With the thunder of Zeus! But by the thunderer's throne
Stood his daughter, the goddess of love, the Graces were standing
  Close by her side! So our bond bears confirmation divine!
Onward hasten, o ship, with all the favoring breezes!
  Onward, powerful keel, cleaving the waves as they foam!
Take me nearer the foreign harbor, and there let the goldsmith
  Toil in his shop, and prepare straightway the heavenly pledge.
Truly the light little chain shall become a chain, o my Dora,
  Nine times circling your neck, loosely around it entwined!
Manifold other adornment I'll buy you; gold-mounted bracelets,
  They shall also grace richly your beautiful arm.
There shall ruby and emerald vie, the sapphire's splendor
  Serve the garnet as foil; all these jewels combined
Shall be held together by gold in a rich combination.
  Oh, how the lover exults when he adorns his betrothed!
Seeing pearls, I think but of you; each ring that I fancy
  Calls to my mind your hand's graceful and tapering form.
I will barter and buy, and you shall choose of the finest,
  Gladly would I devote all of the cargo to you.
But not trinkets and jewels alone your lover will bring you:
  With them he'll bear the things pleasing to housewives as well:
Elegant woollen blankets wrought with an edging of crimson,
  Fit for a couch where both lovingly, gently may rest;
Costly pieces of linen. You sit there sewing and clothing
  Me and yourself and, perhaps, even a third with it too.
Visions of hope, deceive my poor heart! O gods, will you ever
  Dampen this powerful flame rousing a storm in my breast!
Yet I must also crave the return of those rapturous torments
  When Dame Care draws nigh, coldly and horribly calm.
Neither the Furies' torch, nor the hounds of hell with their baying
  Frighten the criminal so down in the realm of despair,
As I am awed by the specter that tranquilly shows me the fair one
  Far away: her gate still, I can see, is ajar!
And another approaches! For him the fruit too is falling,
  And for him also the fig yields its strengthening juice.
Does she entice him as well to the arbor? He follows? Oh, make
  me

Blind, verwischet das Bild jeder Erinnrung in mir!
Ja, ein Mädchen ist sie! und die sich geschwinde dem einen
   Gibt, sie kehret sich auch schnell zu dem andern herum.
Lache nicht diesmal, Zeus, der frech gebrochenen Schwüre!
   Donnere schrecklicher! triff!—Halte die Blitze zurück!
Sende die schwankenden Wolken mir nach! Im nächtlichen Dunkel
   Treffe dein leuchtender Blitz diesen unglücklichen Mast!
Streue die Planken umher und gib der tobenden Welle
   Diese Waren, und mich gib den Delphinen zum Raub!—
Nun, ihr Musen, genug! Vergebens strebt ihr zu schildern,
   Wie sich Jammer und Glück wechseln in liebender Brust.
Heilen könnet die Wunden ihr nicht, die Amor geschlagen;
   Aber Linderung kommt einzig, ihr Guten, von euch.

2. DIE BRAUT VON KORINTH

Nach Korinthus von Athen gezogen
Kam ein Jüngling, dort noch unbekannt.
Einen Bürger hofft' er sich gewogen;
Beide Väter waren gastverwandt,
Hatten frühe schon
Töchterchen und Sohn
Braut und Bräutigam voraus genannt.

Aber wird er auch willkommen scheinen,
Wenn er teuer nicht die Gunst erkauft?
Er ist noch ein Heide mit den Seinen,
Und sie sind schon Christen und getauft.
Keimt ein Glaube neu,
Wird oft Lieb und Treu
Wie ein böses Unkraut ausgerauft.

Und schon lag das ganze Haus im stillen,
Vater, Töchter, nur die Mutter wacht;
Sie empfängt den Gast mit bestem Willen,
Gleich ins Prunkgemach wird er gebracht.
Wein und Essen prangt,
Eh er es verlangt:
So versorgend wünscht sie gute Nacht.

Aber bei dem wohlbestellten Essen
Wird die Lust der Speise nicht erregt;
Müdigkeit lässt Speis und Trank vergessen,

Blind, ye gods, and efface all recollection in me!
Yes, a girl is she! and she who to one will so quickly
    Yield herself up, will ere long turn to another as well.
Laugh not, Zeus, for this once, at oaths so wantonly broken!
    Thunder more fearfully! Strike! Only your lightning withhold!
Send the hovering clouds to me! In the darkness of nighttime,
    Let your lightning's bolt strike this ill-fated mast!
Scatter the planks all around and give to the vehement billows
    All these wares, and *me* give to the dolphins as prey!—
Now, ye Muses, enough! In vain would you strive to uncover
    How in a love-torn breast anguish exchanges with bliss.
Though you cannot heal the wounds by Cupid inflicted,
    Yet all comfort and balm, Kindly Ones, come but from you.

2. THE BRIDE OF CORINTH

Once a youth from Athens had descended
Down to Corinth, unknown there was he;
Hoped a father he would find befriended,
Bound to his in hospitality.
Long the fathers thought
Son and daughter ought
To be joined in wedlock happily.

Will the friendship last, the lad inquires,
If he'll not pay dear for favors prized?
Heathens he and his folks, like their sires,
She and hers are Christians and baptized.
When new faith is born,
Love and troth are torn
Out like weeds and often exorcised.

Father, daughters, they had soon retired,
And alone the mother seeks no rest;
Greets the stranger, by goodwill inspired,
Takes him to the room, the stateliest.
Wine and food are brought
Ere by him they're sought;
Bidding him good night, she leaves the guest.

But he feels no relish for partaking
Of rich food he sees before him spread,
Food and drink in weariness forsaking,

Dass er angekleidet sich aufs Bette legt;
Und er schlummert fast,
Als ein seltner Gast
Sich zur offnen Tür herein bewegt.

Denn er sieht, bei seiner Lampe Schimmer
Tritt, mit weissem Schleier und Gewand,
Sittsam still ein Mädchen in das Zimmer,
Um die Stirn ein schwarz- und goldnes Band.
Wie sie ihn erblickt,
Hebt sie, die erschrickt,
Mit Erstaunen eine weisse Hand.

Bin ich, rief sie aus, so fremd im Hause,
Dass ich von dem Gaste nichts vernahm?
Ach, so hält man mich in meiner Klause!
Und nun überfällt mich hier die Scham.
Ruhe nur so fort
Auf dem Lager dort,
Und ich gehe schnell, so wie ich kam.

Bleibe, schönes Mädchen! ruft der Knabe,
Rafft von seinem Lager sich geschwind:
Hier ist Ceres', hier ist Bacchus' Gabe,
Und du bringst den Amor, liebes Kind!
Bist vor Schrecken blass!
Liebe, komm und lass,
Lass uns sehn, wie froh die Götter sind.

Ferne bleib, o Jüngling! bleibe stehen;
Ich gehöre nicht den Freuden an.
Schon der letzte Schritt ist, ach! geschehen
Durch der guten Mutter kranken Wahn,
Die genesend schwur:
Jugend und Natur
Sei dem Himmel künftig untertan.

Und der alten Götter bunt Gewimmel
Hat sogleich das stille Haus geleert.
Unsichtbar wird Einer nur im Himmel,
Und ein Heiland wird am Kreuz verehrt;
Opfer fallen hier,
Weder Lamm noch Stier,
Aber Menschenopfer unerhört.

Fully clad he lies upon the bed,
Almost sinks to rest
When a strange new guest
Through the open door is seen to tread.

He can see by lamplight dimly burning,
White of veil and robe, a maiden stand
And with decorous footstep toward him turning,
Round her brow a black and golden band.
Sees him where he lies,
Lifts with startled eyes
And astonishment a pallid hand.

Cries: "Just like a stranger would they treat me,
Hide the guest from me! Is that their aim?
Ah, so in my cell they would secrete me!
Now and here I'm overcome with shame.
Slumber on, o guest
On your couch of rest;
I go swiftly, even as I came."

"Stay, o lovely maid!" she hears him crying.
From his couch he rises speedily.
"Ceres' gift and Bacchus' here are lying,
And you, child, bring Cupid on to me!
You are pale with fear,
Dear girl, come, and here
Let us see how joyful gods can be."

"Stay away, o lad, I have forsaken
All these joys, for me they are not meant.
Ah, the final step's already taken
Through my mother's dreams that illness sent,
For she vowed, when healed,
Nature and youth to yield
Up to Heaven, to serve the Lord's intent.

"Soon the old gods' motley swarm was driven
From the quiet house by such disdain.
Worshipped is One God, Unseen, in Heaven,
And a Savior crucified in pain.
Sacrifice is here
Not of lamb nor steer,
But of untold human woe and bane."

Und er fragt und wäget alle Worte,
Deren keines seinem Geist entgeht.
Ist es möglich, dass am stillen Orte
Die geliebte Braut hier vor mir steht?
Sei die Meine nur!
Unsrer Väter Schwur
Hat vom Himmel Segen uns erfleht.

Mich erhältst du nicht, du gute Seele!
Meiner zweiten Schwester gönnt man dich.
Wenn ich mich in stiller Klause quäle,
Ach! in ihren Armen denk an mich,
Die an dich nur denkt,
Die sich liebend kränkt;
In die Erde bald verbirgt sie sich.

Nein! bei dieser Flamme seis geschworen,
Gütig zeigt sie Hymen uns voraus;
Bist der Freude nicht und mir verloren,
Kommst mit mir in meines Vaters Haus.
Liebchen, bleibe hier!
Feire gleich mit mir
Unerwartet unsern Hochzeitschmaus.

Und schon wechseln sie der Treue Zeichen;
Golden reicht sie ihm die Kette dar,
Und er will ihr eine Schale reichen,
Silbern, künstlich, wie nicht eine war.
Die ist nicht für mich;
Doch, ich bitte dich,
Eine Locke gib von deinem Haar.

Eben schlug die dumpfe Geisterstunde,
Und nun schien es ihr erst wohl zu sein.
Gierig schlürfte sie mit blassem Munde
Nun den dunkel blutgefärbten Wein;
Doch vom Weizenbrot,
Das er freundlich bot,
Nahm sie nicht den kleinsten Bissen ein.

Und dem Jüngling reichte sie die Schale,
Der, wie sie, nun hastig lüstern trank.
Liebe fordert er beim stillen Mahle;
Ach, sein armes Herz war liebekrank.

Asking questions, weighing words well tested,
He lets nothing pass his eager ear.
"Can it be that where I should have rested
Came the bride that I have held so dear?
O be mine, dear, now!
Through our fathers' vow
Heaven's blessing has been won us here."

"Me, o gentle soul, you'll not be keeping!
To my sister they would give my place.
When confined in quiet cell I'm weeping,
Think of me if you're in her embrace;
I love you alone
And for love must moan.
'Tis the burial ground I soon must face."

"No and by this flame I firmly swear it,
Which god Hymen shows us, happy pair:
Lost to love and me? I'll never bear it,
To my father's house we will repair.
Stay, o stay, my dear,
Tasting now and here
Of this unexpected bridal fare."

Tokens now to plight their troth they proffer:
And a chain of gold she bids him wear,
While a silver chalice he would offer,
Wrought with cunning art beyond compare.
"'Tis for me no more,
Ah, but I implore,
Give me but a ringlet of your hair."

Dully boomed the witching hour unhallowed,
Now of happier mood she showed a sign.
Eagerly with pallid lips she swallowed
Drafts of dark and rich blood-colored wine;
But on bread of wheat
That he bade her eat
She refused with steadfast will to dine.

To the lad the chalice then she handed
And like her he drank with haste and greed.
Love to crown the feasting he demanded.
How his lovesick heart for love felt need!

Doch sie widersteht,
Wie er immer fleht,
Bis er weinend auf das Bette sank.

   Und sie kommt und wirft sich zu ihm nieder:
Ach, wie ungern seh ich dich gequält!
Aber, ach! berührst du meine Glieder,
Fühlst du schaudernd, was ich dir verhehlt.
Wie der Schnee so weiss,
Aber kalt wie Eis
Ist das Liebchen, das du dir erwählt.

   Heftig fasst er sie mit starken Armen,
Von der Liebe Jugendkraft durchmannt:
Hoffe doch, bei mir noch zu erwarmen,
Wärst du selbst mir aus dem Grab gesandt!
Wechselhauch und Kuss!
Liebesüberfluss!
Brennst du nicht und fühlest mich entbrannt?

   Liebe schliesset fester sie zusammen,
Tränen mischen sich in ihre Lust;
Gierig saugt sie seines Mundes Flammen,
Eins ist nur im andern sich bewusst.
Seine Liebeswut
Wärmt ihr starres Blut,
Doch es schlägt kein Herz in ihrer Brust.

   Unterdessen schleichet auf dem Gange
Häuslich spät die Mutter noch vorbei,
Horchet an der Tür und horchet lange,
Welch ein sonderbarer Ton es sei:
Klag- und Wonnelaut
Bräutigams und Braut,
Und des Liebestammelns Raserei.

   Unbeweglich bleibt sie an der Türe,
Weil sie erst sich überzeugen muss,
Und sie hört die höchsten Liebesschwüre,
Lieb und Schmeichelworte, mit Verdruss—
Still! der Hahn erwacht!—
Aber morgen Nacht
Bist du wieder da?—und Kuss auf Kuss.

But she still resists
While the lad persists.
On the bed he sank in tears to plead.

    To the couch she comes to join her lover:
"Ah, how sadly all your grief I see!
Touch me, though, and, ah, you will discover
What I've hid, and feel it shudderingly.
White as snow on hills,
Cold as ice that chills
Is the sweetheart plighted yours to be."

    And his love he clasps with lover's power,
Youthful passion pulsing through his frame:
"Hope that I will warm you still this hour
E'en if from the grave your spirit came.
Breath for breath, and kiss!
Overflow of bliss
From your ardor feel me all aflame!"

    Tears are mingled with their ardent rapture,
While in love they're close and closer pressed;
From his lips his passion she would capture,
Each is by the other's thought possessed.
Now his passion's flood
Warms her torpid blood,
Yet no heart is beating in her breast.

    But the mother through the hallway hurries,
Softly making wonted rounds, and nears,
Listens at the door where long she tarries,
Wondering at the sounds that greet her ears:
Rapture and despair
From the loving pair,
Passion's stammering ecstasy she hears.

    Motionless before the door she hovers—
She must first convince herself of this—,
When she, vexed, hears ardent vows of lovers,
Coaxing words and sighs of love and bliss.
"Hark, the cock! 'Tis light!"—
"But tomorrow night
You will come again?" And kiss on kiss.

Länger hält die Mutter nicht das Zürnen,
Öffnet das bekannte Schloss geschwind:—
Gibt es hier im Hause solche Dirnen,
Die dem Fremden gleich zu Willen sind?—
So zur Tür hinein.
Bei der Lampe Schein
Sieht sie—Gott! sie sieht ihr eigen Kind.

Und der Jüngling will im ersten Schrecken
Mit des Mädchens eignem Schleierflor,
Mit dem Teppich die Geliebte decken;
Doch sie windet gleich sich selbst hervor.
Wie mit Geists Gewalt
Hebet die Gestalt
Lang und langsam sich im Bett empor.

Mutter! Mutter! spricht sie hohle Worte,
So missgönnt Ihr mir die schöne Nacht!
Ihr vertreibt mich von dem warmen Orte.
Bin ich zur Verzweiflung nur erwacht?
Ists Euch nicht genug,
Dass ins Leichentuch,
Dass Ihr früh mich in das Grab gebracht?

Aber aus der schwerbedeckten Enge
Treibet mich ein eigenes Gericht.
Eurer Priester summende Gesänge
Und ihr Segen haben kein Gewicht;
Salz und Wasser kühlt
Nicht, wo Jugend fühlt;
Ach! die Erde kühlt die Liebe nicht.

Dieser Jüngling war mir erst versprochen,
Als noch Venus' heitrer Tempel stand.
Mutter, habt Ihr doch das Wort gebrochen,
Weil ein fremd, ein falsch Gelübd Euch band!
Doch kein Gott erhört,
Wenn die Mutter schwört,
Zu versagen ihrer Tochter Hand.

Aus dem Grabe werd ich ausgetrieben,
Noch zu suchen das vermisste Gut,
Noch den schon verlornen Mann zu lieben
Und zu saugen seines Herzens Blut.
Ists um den geschehn,

And the mother driven by a nameless
Anger, opens up the door full wide.
"Are there wenches in this house so shameless
To appease the stranger's appetite?"
Through the door she goes,
By the lamp that glows
There—oh God! her daughter meets her sight.

And at first in fright the youthful lover
With her own veil hides the maiden's head,
With the rug his sweetheart he would cover,
But the robe again she soon has shed,
And her form upright
As with spirit's might
Rises full and slowly in the bed.

"Mother!" came her eerie voice, "o tell me,
You begrudge me this night's beauty rare?
From this warming room would you expel me?
Have I wakened only to despair?
Is it not enough
That you drove me off
In an early grave this shroud to wear?

"But from that confinement sealed securely
I am driven by my fate and will.
Murmured chants your priests intone so dourly,
All their blessings can amend no ill;
Salt and water cool
Not when passions rule,
Ah, in earth no youthful love can chill.

"To this youth my pledge had first been spoken,
While the shrine of Venus graced the land.
Then this pledge, o mother, you have broken
Through an alien and false demand.
Wrath no god forbears
When a mother swears
That she'll keep from love a daughter's hand.

"Driven from the grave, I am a rover,
Seeking evermore the ruined Good,
Still to love whom I have lost as lover,
And to suck his heart's most precious blood.
When his life is spent

Muss nach andern gehn,
Und das junge Volk erliegt der Wut.

Schöner Jüngling! kannst nicht länger leben;
Du versiechest nun an diesem Ort.
Meine Kette hab ich dir gegeben;
Deine Locke nehm ich mit mir fort.
Sieh sie an genau!
Morgen bist du grau,
Und nur braun erscheinst du wieder dort.

Höre, Mutter, nun die letzte Bitte:
Einen Scheiterhaufen schichte du;
Öffne meine bange kleine Hütte,
Bring in Flammen Liebende zur Ruh!
Wenn der Funke sprüht,
Wenn die Asche glüht,
Eilen wir den alten Göttern zu.

3. MÄCHTIGES ÜBERRASCHEN

Ein Strom entrauscht umwölktem Felsensaale,
Dem Ozean sich eilig zu verbinden;
Was auch sich spiegeln mag von Grund zu Gründen,
Er wandelt unaufhaltsam fort zu Tale.

Dämonisch aber stürzt mit einem Male—
Ihr folgen Berg und Wald in Wirbelwinden—
Sich Oreas, Behagen dort zu finden,
Und hemmt den Lauf, begrenzt die weite Schale.

Die Welle sprüht und staunt zurück und weichet,
Und schwillt bergan, sich immer selbst zu trinken;
Gehemmt ist nun zum Vater hin das Streben.

Sie schwankt und ruht, zum See zurückgedeichet;
Gestirne, spiegelnd sich, beschaun das Blinken
Des Wellenschlags am Fels, ein neues Leben.

4. DIE LIEBENDE ABERMALS

Warum ich wieder zum Papier mich wende?
Das musst du, Liebster, so bestimmt nicht fragen:
Denn eigentlich hab' ich dir nichts zu sagen;
Doch kommt's zuletzt in deine lieben Hände.

I'll not be content:
All young folk must feel my vampire mood.

"Handsome lad, your span of life is broken,
You will waste, where now you are so fair.
This my chain I gave you as a token,
With me I will take your lock of hair.
See, 'tis brown today,
But tomorrow gray,
You'll no more be brown till over there.

"Listen, mother, hear my last entreaty:
Build a funeral pyre as oft before;
Open up my wretched tomb, for pity,
Let the flames these lovers' peace restore.
When the embers blow,
When the ashes glow,
To the ancient gods we'll swiftly soar."

3. MIGHTY SURPRISE

A stream breaks through its misty caverned pale,
To speed its progress, toward the sea directed;
From depth to depth, whatever is reflected,
It winds its course unchecked into the dale.

A demon lashes up a sudden gale—
By whirlwinds hill and wood are soon affected:—
Nymph Oreas seeks pleasure long expected,
And blocks the stream, and dams the flooded vale.

The billow foams, starts back, begins to break,
And swells uphill, of its own substance drinking;
It cannot reach its goal to Father Ocean.

It falters, rests, impounded as a lake;
Reflected stars look on and see the blinking
Of waves that beat the rocks—new life and motion.

4. THE GIRL WRITES AGAIN TO HER LOVER

Why I resort once more to paper, friend?
Ask not, my dear, with such a searching air!
There really is no news I'd have you share,
But your dear hands will get it in the end.

Weil ich nicht kommen kann, soll, was ich sende,
Mein ungeteiltes Herz hinüber tragen
Mit Wonnen, Hoffnungen, Entzücken, Plagen:
Das alles hat nicht Anfang, hat nicht Ende.

Ich mag vom heut'gen Tag dir nichts vertrauen,
Wie sich im Sinnen, Wünschen, Wähnen, Wollen
Mein treues Herz zu dir hinüber wendet.

So stand ich einst vor dir, dich anzuschauen,
Und sagte nichts. Was hätt' ich sagen sollen?
Mein ganzes Wesen war in sich vollendet.

5. EPOCHE

Mit Flammenschrift war innigst eingeschrieben
Petrarcas Brust, vor allen andern Tagen,
Charfreitag. Eben so, ich darf's wohl sagen,
Ist mir Advent von Achtzehnhundert sieben.

Ich fing nicht an, ich fuhr nur fort zu lieben
Sie, die ich früh im Herzen schon getragen,
Dann wieder weislich aus dem Sinn geschlagen,
Der ich nun wieder bin an's Herz getrieben.

Petrarcas Liebe, die unendlich hohe,
War leider unbelohnt und gar zu traurig,
Ein Herzensweh, ein ewiger Charfreitag;

Doch stets erscheine, fort und fort, die frohe,
Süss, unter Palmenjubel, wonneschaurig,
Der Herrin Ankunft mir, ein ew'ger Maitag.

6. GLEICH UND GLEICH

Ein Blumenglöckchen
Vom Boden hervor
War früh gesprosset
In lieblichem Flor;
Da kam ein Bienchen
Und naschte fein:-
Die müssen wohl beide
Für einander sein.

Because I cannot come, whate'er I send
My undivided heart to you shall bear
With ecstasy, hope, rapture, and despair.
All that has no beginning, has no end.

And of this day I'd give you not a clue
How I, to brooding, craving, dreaming bred,
Have turned my heart to you with every beat.

'Tis thus I faced you once, to gaze on you,
But nothing said. And what should I have said?
For in itself my being was complete.

5. EPOCH

Engraved in letters that by flames were wrought,
Good Friday blazed bright as no other day
In Petrarch's breast. To me, I well may say,
Advent in eighteen 'seven surpasses aught.

I did not start but kept up loving thought
Of her who early in my heart held sway,
Then, prudent, put her from my thoughts away,
To whom I once again am closer brought.

The love that Petrarch sang, nobly divine,
Was unrequited, all too melancholy,
A heartache, and an endless sad Good Friday;

To me shall Advent ever happy shine,
Sweet among joyous palms, ecstatic-holy,
My lady's Advent, May's undying high-day.

6. LIKE AND LIKE

A bell-shaped flower
Sprang up from the ground
And blossomed early,
By loveliness crowned.
A bee came flitting
And sipped unafraid.
For one another
They must have been made.

7. KRITTLER

Ein unverschämter Naseweis,
Der, was er durch Stahlarbeitersfleiss
Auf dem Laden künstlich liegen sah,
Dacht', es wär' für ihn alleine da:
So tatscht' er dem geduldigen Mann
Die blanken Waren sämtlich an
Und schätzte sie, nach Dünkelsrecht,
Das Schlechte hoch, das Gute schlecht,
Getrost, zufriednen Angesichts;
Dann ging er weg und kaufte nichts.

Den Kramer das zuletzt verdross,
Und macht ein stählern künstlich Schloss
Zur rechten Stunde glühend heiss.
Da ruft gleich unser Naseweis:
„Wer wird so schlechte Ware kaufen!
Der Stahl ist schändlich angelaufen."
Und tappt auch gleich recht läppisch drein
Und fängt erbärmlich an zu schrein.
Der Kramer fragt: was ist denn das?
Der Quidam schreit: „Ein frostiger Spass!"

8. POESIE

Gott sandte seinen rohen Kindern
Gesetz und Ordnung, Wissenschaft und Kunst,
Begabte die mit aller Himmelsgunst,
Der Erde grasses Los zu mindern.
Sie kamen nackt vom Himmel an
Und wussten sich nicht zu benehmen;
Die Poesie zog ihnen Kleider an,
Und keine hatte sich zu schämen.

9. URWORTE. ORPHISCH

ΔΑΙΜΩΝ, Dämon

Wie an dem Tag, der dich der Welt verliehen,
Die Sonne stand zum Grusse der Planeten,
Bist alsobald und fort und fort gediehen
Nach dem Gesetz, wonach du angetreten.
So musst du sein, dir kannst du nicht entfliehen,

7. FAULT FINDER

An impudent and prying bore
Who, sauntering through a hardware store,
Saw handsome wares upon the shelf,
Thought they were there but for himself.
So, while the suffering merchant lingered,
The polished wares this rascal fingered,
Appraising, as all fools will try,
The fine things low, the poor things high,
With confident, contented mien,
Then, buying nothing, left the scene.

At last he roused the merchant's ire,
Who laid a steel lock in the fire
And made it hot and glowing red.
Just then the boor returned and said:
"Who'd sell such trash as this to me?
The steel is tarnished shamefully!"
With clumsy hand he grasped the lock
And then he voiced his painful shock.
"What's troubling you?" the merchant called.
"A frosty joke!" the rascal bawled.

8. POETRY

God sent his children in raw estate
Both law and order, science too and art,
With Heaven's favor setting them apart,
To lighten the earth's crass, cruel fate.
They came from heaven naked and bare
And acted ill-behaved, untamed;
Then poetry gave them clothes to wear,
And none had cause to be ashamed.

9. PRIMAL WORDS. ORPHIC

Daimon (Demon)

As on that day which blessed the world with thee
The sun stood high to send the planets greeting,
Thou soon didst thrive and prosper constantly,
According to the law that gave thee being.
So must thou be, thyself thou canst not flee,

So sagten schon Sibyllen, so Propheten;
Und keine Zeit und keine Macht zerstückelt
Geprägte Form, die lebend sich entwickelt.

TYXH, das Zufällige

Die strenge Grenze doch umgeht gefällig
Ein Wandelndes, das mit und um uns wandelt;
Nicht einsam bleibst du, bildest dich gesellig,
Und handelst wohl so, wie ein andrer handelt:
Im Leben ists bald hin-, bald widerfällig,
Es ist ein Tand und wird so durchgetandelt.
Schon hat sich still der Jahre Kreis geründet,
Die Lampe harrt der Flamme, die entzündet.

EPΩΣ, Liebe

Die bleibt nicht aus!—Er stürzt vom Himmel nieder,
Wohin er sich aus alter Öde schwang,
Er schwebt heran auf luftigem Gefieder
Um Stirn und Brust den Frühlingstag entlang,
Scheint jetzt zu fliehn, vom Fliehen kehrt er wieder:
Da wird ein Wohl im Weh, so süss und bang.
Gar manches Herz verschwebt in Allgemeinen,
Doch widmet sich das edelste dem Einen.

ANAΓKH, Nötigung

Da ists denn wieder, wie die Sterne wollten:
Bedingung und Gesetz; und aller Wille
Ist nur ein Wollen, weil wir eben sollten,
Und vor dem Willen schweigt die Willkür stille;
Das Liebste wird vom Herzen weggescholten,
Dem harten Muss bequemt sich Will und Grille.
So sind wir scheinfrei denn, nach manchen Jahren
Nur enger dran, als wir am Anfang waren.

EΛΠΙΣ, Hoffnung

Doch solcher Grenze, solcher ehrnen Mauer
Höchst widerwärtge Pforte wird entriegelt,
Sie stehe nur mit alter Felsendauer!
Ein Wesen regt sich leicht und ungezügelt:
Aus Wolkendecke, Nebel, Regenschauer
Erhebt sie uns, mit ihr, durch sie beflügelt,
Ihr kennt sie wohl, sie schwärmt durch alle Zonen—
Ein Flügelschlag—und hinter uns Äonen!

So Sibyls, Prophets long have been decreeing.
No time, no power ever has dissolved
Fixed types that have as living forms evolved.

Tyche (Chance)

But change that changes with and o'er us all
Slips by those barriers and pushes through.
Thou stayest not alone, art sociable,
Acting as any other one would do.
In life it fluctuates mid rise and fall,
A bauble, and as such 'tis dawdled through.
The cycle of the years has crept its rounds,
The lamp awaits the flame that upwards bounds.

Eros (Love)

It cannot fail! From heaven Love doth rain,
Whence out of primal void he made his way,
On gentle wings he reaches us amain
Round head and heart along the springtime day,
He seems to flee and soon appears again.
Then joys in woe sweet-fearfully hold sway.
'Mongst many some hearts scatter love's emotion,
The noblest though pays One its full devotion.

Anagke (Necessity)

Once more 'thas come as stars decree it would:
Necessity and Law; and all our Will
Is only Will because 'tis said we should,
And faced by Will, all license must be still.
What most we love, we're chided, can't be good.
"Thou shalt" dictates what whims must needs fulfill:
Delusive freedom after many an inning
Confines us closer than at our beginning.

Elpis (Hope)

At last the hated portal must unlock,
Permitting us to pass the brazen wall.
O let it stand, this old eternal rock!
A creature stirs, not meekly held in thrall.
No cloud or fog or rain can hem or block
Our course, with Hope we're winged above the pall—
Ye know her well, she swarms through every region—
A flap of wings! behind us years in legion.

10. MÄRZ

Es ist ein Schnee gefallen,
Denn es ist noch nicht Zeit,
Dass von den Blümlein allen,
Dass von den Blümlein allen
Wir werden hoch erfreut.

Der Sonnenblick betrüget
Mit mildem, falschem Schein,
Die Schwalbe selber lüget,
Die Schwalbe selber lüget,
Warum? Sie kommt allein!

Sollt ich mich einzeln freuen,
Wenn auch der Frühling nah?
Doch kommen wir zu zweien,
Doch kommen wir zu zweien,
Gleich ist der Sommer da.

10. MARCH

The snow has come in showers,
For it is not yet time
That we by all the flowers,
That we by all the flowers
Be filled with joy sublime.

With fraudulent desire
The sun's mild rays have shone,
The swallow is a liar,
The swallow is a liar.
And why? He comes alone.

Though now there'll be spring weather,
Can I, alone, find cheer?
But once we're two together,
But once we're two together,
Summer will soon be here.

CHAPTER V. FROM THE "WEST-EASTERLY DIVAN".

TALISMANE

1. Er, der einzige Gerechte,
   Will für jedermann das Rechte.
   Sei von seinen hundert Namen
   Dieser hochgelobet! Amen.

2. Ob ich Irdsches denk und sinne,
   Das gereicht zu höherem Gewinne.
   Mit dem Staube nicht der Geist zerstoben,
   Dringet, in sich selbst gedrängt, nach oben.

BUCH DER SPRÜCHE

3. Wenn der schwer Gedrückte klagt:
   Hilfe, Hoffnung sei versagt,
   Bleibet heilsam fort und fort
   Immer noch ein freundlich Wort.

* * *

4. Gesteht's! Die Dichter des Orients
   Sind grösser als wir des Okzidents.
   Worin wir sie aber völlig erreichen,
   Das ist im Hass auf unseresgleichen.

* * *

5. Soll man dich nicht aufs schmählichste berauben,
   Verbirg dein Gold, dein Weggehn, deinen Glauben.

6. SULEIKA 1.

Suleika

Volk und Knecht und Überwinder
Sie gestehn, zu jeder Zeit:
Höchstes Glück der Erdenkinder
Sei nur die Persönlichkeit.

Jedes Leben sei zu führen,
Wenn man sich nicht selbst vermisst;
Alles könne man verlieren,
Wenn man bliebe, was man ist.

TALISMANS

1. He, the only Righteous One
   Wills the right for everyone:
   This name, of his hundred, then,
   Shall be highly praised! Amen.

2. Ever higher gain it brings
   When I contemplate the earthly things.
   Not like dust is spirit extirpated,
   But will rise to heaven, concentrated.

BOOK OF SAYINGS

3. When the hard oppressed complain
   That no help and hope remain,
   Still one blessing may be heard:
   A kindly spoken, friendly word.

   * * *

4. Admit it that the eastern poets
   Surpass us who are western poets.
   But in one matter we're peers, I find:
   In hatred of our identical kind.

   * * *

5. If you would not be robbed in shameful scathe,
   Guard well your gold, your parting and your faith.

6. SULEIKA 1.

Suleika
Folk and slave and subjugator
Will admit it readily:
Children of earth have no boons greater
Than their personality.

Any life should satisfy you
If yourself you'll not disdain,
Many things let fate deny you,
But yourself you must remain.

Hatem

Kann wohl sein! so wird gemeinet;
Doch ich bin auf andrer Spur:
Alles Erdenglück vereinet
Find' ich in Suleika nur.

Wie sie sich an mich verschwendet,
Bin ich mir ein wertes Ich;
Hätte sie sich weggewendet,
Augenblicks verlör' ich mich.

Nun mit Hatem wär's zu Ende;
Doch schon hab' ich umgelost:
Ich verkörpre mich behende
In den Holden, den sie kost.

Wollte, wo nicht gar ein Rabbi,
Das will mir so recht nicht ein,
Doch Ferdusi, Montanabbi,
Allenfalls der Kaiser sein.

7. HATEM

Locken, haltet mich gefangen
In dem Kreise des Gesichts!
Euch geliebten braunen Schlangen
Zu erwidern hab' ich nichts.

Nur dies Herz, es ist von Dauer,
Schwillt in jugendlichstem Flor;
Unter Schnee und Nebelschauer
Rast ein Ätna dir hervor.

Du beschämst wie Morgenröte
Jener Gipfel ernste Wand,
Und noch einmal fühlet Hatem
Frühlingshauch und Sommerbrand.

Schenke her! Noch eine Flasche!
Diesen Becher bring' ich ihr!
Findet sie ein Häufchen Asche,
Sagt sie: der verbrannte mir.

Hatem

That may be! 'tis often stated,
But I've something else in mind.
Earth's delights, all concentrated,
I in my Suleika find.

When she gives me all her loving,
How my ego comes to flower!
But if she had turned to roving,
I would lose myself that hour.

Then with Hatem 'twould be ended,
But already I'm converted.
I transform myself, soon blended
With the swain with whom she's flirted.

I would be, if not a rabbi
(This I'm scarcely suited for),
Yet Ferduse, Montanabbi,
Or perhaps the emperor.

7. HATEM

Locks, enthrall and captivate me,
As around her face you flow!
Snakes of brown that fascinate me,
Naught like these have I to show.

But this heart, with lasting powers,
Swells and blooms most youthfully;
Under snow and fog in showers
Etna's fury you can see.

Like the dawn you shame and humble
All the hilltops' towering height,
And once more there come to Hatem
Springtime's breath and summer's might.

Pour! A new flask! Yes, another!
And to her I'll pledge the cup!
If she sees an ash-heap smother,
Love, she'll say, has burned him up.

8. SULEIKA 2.

Nimmer will ich dich verlieren!
Liebe gibt der Liebe Kraft.
Magst du meine Jugend zieren
Mit gewalt'ger Leidenschaft.
Ach! Wie schmeichelt's meinem Triebe,
Wenn man meinen Dichter preist.
Denn das Leben ist die Liebe,
Und des Lebens Leben Geist.

9. SULEIKA 3.

Was bedeutet die Bewegung?
Bringt der Ost mir frohe Kunde?
Seiner Schwingen frische Regung
Kühlt des Herzens tiefe Wunde.

Kosend spielt er mit dem Staube,
Jagt ihn auf in leichten Wölkchen,
Treibt zur sichern Rebenlaube
Der Insekten frohes Völkchen.

Lindert sanft der Sonne Glühen,
Kühlt auch mir die heissen Wangen,
Küsst die Reben noch im Fliehen,
Die auf Feld und Hügel prangen.

Und mir bringt sein leises Flüstern
Von dem Freunde tausend Grüsse;
Eh' noch diese Hügel düstern,
Grüssen mich wohl tausend Küsse.

Und so kannst du weiter ziehen!
Diene Freunden und Betrübten.
Dort, wo hohe Mauern glühen,
Find' ich bald den Vielgeliebten.

Ach, die wahre Herzenskunde,
Liebeshauch, erfrischtes Leben
Wird mir nur aus seinem Munde,
Kann mir nur sein Atem geben.

10. WIEDERFINDEN

Ist es möglich! Stern der Sterne,

8. SULEIKA 2.

Never would I lose you, lover!
Love gives love the strength to grow,
Help my youth new charms uncover
With a passion that's aglow.
Ah, with pride my heart's unruly
When my poet's praise I hear.
"Life is love" was spoken truly,
And life's life is spirit, dear.

9. SULEIKA 3.

Why this tumult, why this stirring?
Does the East bring words of balm?
With his wings' refreshful whirring
Soon my wounded heart is calm.

East wind with the dust is jesting,
Driving wisps of it along,
And in grapevines harbors nesting
Insects in a happy throng,

Gently stills the sun's bright ardor,
Cools my heated cheeks for me,
Kisses vines while fleeing farther,
Which on hills grow radiantly.

East wind's whispering brings my lover's
Countless thoughts of love to greet me,
And ere night these hilltops covers
Endless kisses come to meet me.

Move ahead in your desire!
Serve your friends and those oppressed.
Soon where lofty walls rise higher
In my lover's arms I'll rest.

Ah, the tidings hearts can proffer,
Sighs of love and life aglow,
These, his lips alone can offer,
His breath only can bestow.

10. REDISCOVERY

Star of stars; o can it be!

Drück' ich wieder dich ans Herz!
Ach, was ist die Nacht der Ferne
Für ein Abgrund, für ein Schmerz!
Ja, du bist es, meiner Freuden
Süsser, lieber Widerpart;
Eingedenk vergangner Leiden,
Schaudr' ich vor der Gegenwart.

 Als die Welt im tiefsten Grunde
Lag an Gottes ew'ger Brust,
Ordnet' er die erste Stunde
Mit erhabner Schöpfungslust,
Und er sprach das Wort: Es werde!
Da erklang ein schmerzlich Ach!
Als das All mit Machtgebärde
In die Wirklichkeiten brach.

 Auf tat sich das Licht: so trennte
Scheu sich Finsternis von ihm,
Und sogleich die Elemente
Scheidend auseinander fliehn.
Rasch, in wilden, wüsten Träumen
Jedes nach der Weite rang,
Starr, in ungemessnen Räumen,
Ohne Sehnsucht, ohne Klang.

 Stumm war alles, still und öde,
Einsam Gott zum erstenmal!
Da erschuf er Morgenröte,
Die erbarmte sich der Qual;
Sie entwickelte dem Trüben
Ein erklingend Farbenspiel,
Und nun konnte wieder lieben,
Was erst auseinander fiel.

 Und mit eiligem Bestreben
Sucht sich, was sich angehört;
Und zu ungemessnem Leben
Ist Gefühl und Blick gekehrt.
Sei's Ergreifen, sei es Raffen,
Wenn es sich nur fasst und hält!
Allah braucht nicht mehr zu schaffen,
Wir erschaffen seine Welt.

Are you in my arms again?
Ah, when you are far from me,
What abysmal night of pain!
You, the foe of all my gladness,
My tormentor sweet and dear;
Thinking of my bygone sadness,
'Tis the present that I fear.

When the world and all its dower
Lay on God's eternal breast,
He arranged the primal hour
With a high creative zest.
His "So be it" did He utter,
Anguished cries rang painfully
When the cosmos' mighty flutter
Burst into reality.

Light shot forth, and flying hence,
Off did darkness shyly dart,
And forthwith the elements
Leave their home to live apart.
Swift, by dreams of madness hounded,
Each one wrestled to be free,
Rigid and in space unbounded,
Yearningless and silently.

Mute was all, and hushed and dead,
Ne'er had God such lonesome reign!
Then He made the morning red,
Which took pity upon this pain.
Ringing colors did it nourish,
Cloudiness must soon depart,
Love and harmony could flourish
'Mongst what just had burst apart.

Creatures all with hurried striving
Seek their own affinity,
And to full unmeasured living
Heart and eye turn eagerly.
Seized or snatched, howe'er you state it,
'Tmust be held whate'er is caught!
Allah need no more create it,
We'll create the world he's sought.

So, mit morgenroten Flügeln,
Riss es mich an deinen Mund,
Und die Nacht mit tausend Siegeln
Kräftigt sternenhell den Bund.
Beide sind wir auf der Erde
Musterhaft in Freud' und Qual,
Und ein zweites Wort: Es werde!
Trennt uns nicht zum zweitenmal.

11. VOLLMONDNACHT

Herrin, sag', was heisst das Flüstern?
Was bewegt dir leis die Lippen?
Lispelst immer vor dich hin,
Lieblicher als Weines Nippen!
Denkst du, deinen Mundgeschwistern
Noch ein Pärchen herzuziehn?

„Ich will küssen! Küssen! sagt' ich."

Schau'! Im zweifelhaften Dunkel
Glühen blühend alle Zweige,
Nieder spielet Stern auf Stern;
Und smaragden durchs Gesträuche
Tausendfältiger Karfunkel:
Doch dein Geist ist allem fern.

„Ich will küssen! Küssen! sagt' ich."

Dein Geliebter, fern, erprobet
Gleicherweis' im Sauersüssen,
Fühlt ein unglücksel'ges Glück.
Euch im Vollmond zu begrüssen,
Habt ihr heilig angelobet;
Dieses ist der Augenblick.

„Ich will küssen! Küssen! sag' ich."

12.

Die Welt durchaus ist lieblich anzuschauen,
Vorzüglich aber schön die Welt der Dichter,
Auf bunten, hellen oder silbergrauen
Gefilden, Tag und Nacht, erglänzen Lichter.

So with dawn-red wings in flight
To your kisses I was driven;
With a thousand seals the night
Knits our bonds 'neath starry heaven.
Both of us on earth betoken
Earthly joy and earthly pain.
That creative word, re-spoken,
Shall divide us not again.

11. FULL MOON NIGHT

Why these whispered words, my mistress,
From your lips so softly slipping,
Whispered words that you repeat?
Lovelier than wine in sipping!
Do your mouth's two ruby sisters
Crave two lips that yours could meet?

"I would kiss! Yes, kiss, I told you."

See in this uncertain gloom
Every branch in blowing glows,
Starry light reflects on star;
A thousandfold carbuncle shows
Emerald hues where bushes loom:
But from this your mind is far.

"I would kiss! Yes, kiss, I told you."

But your faroff lover, skilled
Just as well in bitter-sweet,
Feels an unpropitious bliss.
In the full of moon you'd meet,
That is what you vowed and willed;
Now the time has come for this.

"I would kiss! Yes, kiss, I'm saying."

12.

The world is fair to view where'er we stray,
The world of poets though supremely bright.
On fields of color, clear or silvery gray,
High lights are radiant by day and night.

Heut ist mir alles herrlich; wenns nur bliebe!
Ich sehe heut durchs Augenglas der Liebe.

13.

In welchem Weine
Hat sich Alexander betrunken?
Ich wette den letzten Lebensfunken:
Er war nicht so gut als der meine.

To me all's glorious today, let it not pass!
Today I'm looking through a lover's glass.

13.

What brand of wine
Caused Alexander's brain to seethe?
I'd bet the final breath I breathe
That it wasn't as good as mine.

CHAPTER VI. LATE POEMS AND EPIGRAMS

1. PARABASE

Freudig war, vor vielen Jahren,
Eifrig so der Geist bestrebt,
Zu erforschen, zu erfahren,
Wie Natur im Schaffen lebt.
Und es ist das ewig Eine,
Das sich vielfach offenbart:
Klein das Grosse, gross das Kleine,
Alles nach der eignen Art;
Immer wechselnd, fest sich haltend,
Nah und fern und fern und nah,
So gestaltend, umgestaltend—
Zum Erstaunen bin ich da.

2. EPIRRHEMA

Müsset im Naturbetrachten
Immer eins wie alles achten:
Nichts ist drinnen, nichts ist draussen;
Denn was innen, das ist aussen.
So ergreifet ohne Säumnis
Heilig öffentlich Geheimnis.

Freuet euch des wahren Scheins,
Euch des ernsten Spieles:
Kein Lebendiges ist ein Eins,
Immer ists ein Vieles.

3. ANTEPIRRHEMA

So schauet mit bescheidnem Blick
Der ewigen Weberin Meisterstück,
Wie Ein Tritt tausend Fäden regt,
Die Schifflein hinüber herüber schiessen,
Die Fäden sich begegnend fliessen,
Ein Schlag tausend Verbindungen schlägt,
Das hat sie nicht zusammen gebettelt,
Sie hat's von Ewigkeit angezettelt;
Damit der ewige Meistermann
Getrost den Einschlag werfen kann.

1. PARABASIS

Joyful many years ago
Did the Spirit use his powers
To examine and to know
How creative nature flowers.
'Tis the eternal One and All,
Variously revealed, I find:
Small the great and great the small,
Each according to its kind;
Given to change, and then duration,
Near and far, and far and near,
Shaping form, then transformation—
'Tis for wonderment I'm here.

2. EPIRRHEMA

Students of nature, make this your goal:
Heed the specimen, heed the Whole.
Nothing is inside or out,
What's within must outward sprout.
So without delay one sees
Sacred open mysteries.

Truth in semblance never shun,
Solemn sport uphold,
What's alive cannot be One,
It's always manifold.

3. ANTEPIRRHEMA

And so behold with humility
The eternal Weaver's mastery:
How one thrust stirs up thread on thread,
And back and forth the shuttles go,
While threads are meeting as they flow,
And countless networks obey one tread.
This was not begged from door to door,
Thus she arranged it forevermore,
So that the Master, who is deft,
May calmly regulate the weft.

4. ULTIMATUM

Und so sag' ich zum letzten Male:
Natur hat weder Kern
Noch Schale;
Du prüfe dich nur allermeist,
Ob du Kern oder Schale seist!

„Wir kennen dich, du Schalk!
Du machst nur Possen;
Vor unsrer Nase doch
Ist viel verschlossen."

Ihr folget falscher Spur,
Denkt nicht wir scherzen!
Ist nicht der Kern der Natur
Menschen im Herzen?

5-7. TRILOGIE DER LEIDENSCHAFT

(5) 1. An Werther

Noch einmal wagst du, vielbeweinter Schatten,
Hervor dich an das Tageslicht,
Begegnest mir auf neu beblümten Matten,
Und meinen Anblick scheust du nicht.
Es ist, als ob du lebtest in der Frühe,
Wo uns der Tau auf Einem Feld erquickt
Und nach des Tages unwillkommner Mühe
Der Scheidesonne letzter Strahl entzückt;
Zum Bleiben ich, zum Scheiden du erkoren,
Gingst du voran—und hast nicht viel verloren.

Des Menschen Leben scheint ein herrlich Los:
Der Tag wie lieblich, so die Nacht wie gross!
Und wir, gepflanzt in Paradieses Wonne,
Geniessen kaum der hocherlauchten Sonne,
Da kämpft sogleich verworrene Bestrebung
Bald mit uns selbst und bald mit der Umgebung;
Keins wird vom andern wünschenswert ergänzt,
Von aussen düsterts, wenn es innen glänzt,
Ein glänzend Äussres deckt ein trüber Blick,
Da steht es nah—und man verkennt das Glück.

4. ULTIMATUM

So for the last time mark it well:
Nature has neither kernel
Nor shell;
Now test yourself most carefully
Whether kernel or shell you be.

"We know you well, you wag!
You are not serious;
Before our very nose
Much is concealed from us."

Your scent is all awry,
Think not that we jest!
Does nature's kernel not lie
In mankind's breast?

5-7. TRILOGY OF PASSION

(5) 1. To Werther

Once more you venture, much lamented shadow,
To issue forth into the sun,
You meet me on a newly flowering meadow,
The sight of me you would not shun.
It seems as though at early dawn you're living,
When on one field the dewdrops sparkle bright
And at the end of day's unwelcome striving
The sinking sun's last ray affords delight;
For staying I, for parting you were meant.
You've lost but little, as ahead you went.

Man's life appears to be a glorious fate:
The day how lovely, so the night how great!
And we, planted in joys of Paradise,
The high, illustrious sun can scarcely prize!
At once disordered striving seems content
To clash with us and our environment;
None supplements the other, as is right,
Outside comes darkness, while within is light,
A gloomy look conceals an outer glow,
It's near—but happiness we fail to know.

Nun glauben wirs zu kennen! Mit Gewalt
Ergreift uns Liebreiz weiblicher Gestalt:
Der Jüngling, froh wie in der Kindheit Flor,
Im Frühling tritt als Frühling selbst hervor,
Entzückt, erstaunt, wer dies ihm angetan?
Er schaut umher, die Welt gehört ihm an.
Ins Weite zieht ihn unbefangne Hast,
Nichts engt ihn ein, nicht Mauer, nicht Palast;
Wie Vögelschar an Wäldergipfeln streift,
So schwebt auch er, der um die Liebste schweift,
Er sucht vom Äther, den er gern verlässt,
Den treuen Blick, und dieser hält ihn fest.

Doch erst zu früh und dann zu spät gewarnt,
Fühlt er den Flug gehemmt, fühlt sich umgarnt.
Das Wiedersehn ist froh, das Scheiden schwer,
Das Wieder-Wiedersehn beglückt noch mehr,
Und Jahre sind im Augenblick ersetzt;
Doch tückisch harrt das Lebewohl zuletzt.

Du lächelst, Freund, gefühlvoll, wie sich ziemt:
Ein grässlich Scheiden machte dich berühmt;
Wir feierten dein kläglich Missgeschick,
Du liessest uns zu Wohl und Weh zurück.
Dann zog uns wieder ungewisse Bahn
Der Leidenschaften labyrinthisch an;
Und wir, verschlungen wiederholter Not,
Dem Scheiden endlich—Scheiden ist der Tod!
Wie klingt es rührend, wenn der Dichter singt,
Den Tod zu meiden, den das Scheiden bringt!
Verstrickt in solche Qualen, halbverschuldet,
Geb ihm ein Gott, zu sagen, was er duldet.

(6) 2. Elegie

Und wenn der Mensch in seiner Qual verstummt,
Gab mir ein Gott zu sagen, was ich leide.

Was soll ich nun vom Wiedersehen hoffen,
Von dieses Tages noch geschlossner Blüte?
Das Paradies, die Hölle steht dir offen;
Wie wankelsinnig regt sich's im Gemüte!—

At last we think we know! With mighty power
We're seized by charms of woman's form and flower:
The youth again in childhood's bloom is gay,
In spring comes forth as spring to greet the day,
Delighted and surprised, who wrought such bliss?
He looks about and all the world is his.
In artless haste he roams the world and all,
Is not confined by palace nor by wall;
Like birds that over wooded hilltops hover,
So flutters he who hovers round his lover,
Seeking from ether, which he likes to flee,
A faithful eye, that holds him mightily.

First warned too early, then not soon enough,
His flight is checked by nets he cannot slough.
Reunion cheers him, but the parting's sore,
Though re-reunion cheers him even more,
And many years are compensated fast;
But tricky lurks the leave he takes at last.

You smile with feeling, friend, to suit your name:
Your horrible departure brought you fame;
Your mournful fate gave rise to celebration,
You left us here for weal and lamentation,
And then an unsure path of passions drew
Us in a labyrinthine course anew;
And we, often consumed by grief and sighs,
And last by parting—who must part, he dies!
Heart-breaking 'tis whene'er the poet sings
To flee from death that such leave-taking brings!
Caught in such tortures—half the blame he shares—,
May some god let him speak the woe he bears.

(6) 2. Elegy

And when in all his torture man grows mute
A god gave me the strength to tell my suff'ring.

What shall I hope when she again may meet me,
What hope in this day's bud that still is closed?
Both Paradise and Hell unbolt to greet me;
To indecision is my soul disposed!

Kein Zweifeln mehr! Sie tritt ans Himmelstor,
Zu ihren Armen hebt sie dich empor.

*

So warst du denn im Paradies empfangen,
Als wärst du wert des ewig schönen Lebens;
Dir blieb kein Wunsch, kein Hoffen, kein Verlangen,
Hier war das Ziel des innigsten Bestrebens,
Und in dem Anschaun dieses einzig Schönen
Versiegte gleich der Quell sehnsüchtiger Tränen.

Wie regte nicht der Tag die raschen Flügel,
Schien die Minuten vor sich her zu treiben!
Der Abendkuss, ein treu verbindlich Siegel:
So wird es auch der nächsten Sonne bleiben.
Die Stunden glichen sich in zartem Wandern
Wie Schwestern zwar, doch keine ganz den andern.

Der Kuss, der letzte, grausam süss, zerschneidend
Ein herrliches Geflecht verschlungner Minnen—
Nun eilt, nun stockt der Fuss, die Schwelle meidend,
Als trieb' ein Cherub flammend ihn von hinnen;
Das Auge starrt auf düstrem Pfad verdrossen,
Es blickt zurück: die Pforte steht verschlossen.

Und nun verschlossen in sich selbst, als hätte
Dies Herz sich nie geöffnet, selige Stunden
Mit jedem Stern des Himmels um die Wette
An ihrer Seite leuchtend nicht empfunden;
Und Missmut, Reue, Vorwurf, Sorgenschwere
Belasten's nun in schwüler Atmosphäre.

Ist denn die Welt nicht übrig? Felsenwände,
Sind sie nicht mehr gekrönt von heiligen Schatten?
Die Ernte, reift sie nicht? Ein grün Gelände,
Zieht sich's nicht hin am Fluss durch Busch und Matten?
Und wölbt sich nicht das überweltlich Grosse,
Gestaltenreiche, bald Gestaltenlose?

Wie leicht und zierlich, klar und zart gewoben
Schwebt, seraphgleich, aus ernster Wolken Chor,
Als glich' es ihr, am blauen Äther droben
Ein schlank Gebild aus lichtem Duft empor;

No doubt remains! The gates of heaven she faces
And lifts me up to be in her embraces.

*

And so in Paradise you were received,
As though you'd earned ideal life forever;
No wish, desire or hope was now deceived,
Here was attained the goal of fond endeavor,
And by the sight of such rare beauty thrilled,
My spring of yearning tears was quickly stilled.

How clearly day's swift winging we could feel,
Which drove the minutes forward as it flew!
The evening kiss, a true and binding seal.
So will the next day's dawning find it too.
The hours in tender course, like one another,
Seemed sisters, yet they differed from each other.

That kiss, the last one, sweet but cruel, tore
A glorious web of love that held us tight—
My hastening foot now stops, avoids her door,
As though barred by a cherub flaming bright;
My eye stares vexed upon its path of gloom,
Backward it looks and sees a bolted room.

With bolt upon this heart, as if it too
Had never opened wide and never shared
A rivalled bliss with every star it knew,
When beaming at the loved one's side I fared;
Ill humor, rue, reproach, depression drear
Now weigh it down in sultry atmosphere.

Does not the world remain? Cliffs high and wide,
Are they no longer crowned by sacred shadows?
Does not the crop mature? Green countryside,
Does it not roll by streams, through bush and meadows?
Is not the vaulting firmament still there,
And things of shape that soon of shape are bare?

How light and graceful, clear and tender wove,
From choirs of clouds a seraph comes to view,
As though like her, from gentle haze above,
A slender form emerging in the blue!

So sahst du sie in frohem Tanze walten,
Die lieblichste der lieblichsten Gestalten.

Doch nur Momente darfst dich unterwinden,
Ein Luftgebild statt ihrer festzuhalten;
Ins Herz zurück! dort wirst du's besser finden,
Dort regt sie sich in wechselnden Gestalten:
Zu vielen bildet Eine sich hinüber,
So tausendfach, und immer, immer lieber.

Wie zum Empfang sie an den Pforten weilte
Und mich von dannauf stufenweis beglückte,
Selbst nach dem letzten Kuss mich noch ereilte,
Den letztesten mir auf die Lippen drückte:
So klar beweglich bleibt das Bild der Lieben
Mit Flammenschrift ins treue Herz geschrieben.

Ins Herz, das fest, wie zinnenhohe Mauer
Sich ihr bewahrt und sie in sich bewahret,
Für sie sich freut an seiner eignen Dauer,
Nur weiss von sich, wenn sie sich offenbaret,
Sich freier fühlt in so geliebten Schranken
Und nur noch schlägt, für alles ihr zu danken.

War Fähigkeit zu lieben, war Bedürfen
Von Gegenliebe weggelöscht, verschwunden,
Ist Hoffnungslust zu freudigen Entwürfen,
Entschlüssen, rascher Tat sogleich gefunden!
Wenn Liebe je den Liebenden begeistet,
Ward es an mir aufs lieblichste geleistet;

Und zwar durch sie!—Wie lag ein innres Bangen
Auf Geist und Körper, unwillkommner Schwere,
Von Schauerbildern rings der Blick umfangen
Im wüsten Raum beklommner Herzensleere;
Nun dämmert Hoffnung von bekannter Schwelle:
Sie selbst erscheint in milder Sonnenhelle.

Dem Frieden Gottes, welcher euch hienieden
Mehr als Vernunft beseliget—wir lesen's—
Vergleich' ich wohl der Liebe heitern Frieden
In Gegenwart des allgeliebten Wesens;
Da ruht das Herz, und nichts vermag zu stören
Den tiefsten Sinn: den Sinn, ihr zu gehören.

Thus did you see her joyously advance,
The fairest of the fairest in the dance.

For moments only you, a daring lover,
May hold a vision fast instead of her;
Look in your heart! There better you'll discover
Where she in ever changing forms doth stir;
One takes the shape of many ever clearer,
So thousandfold, and ever, ever dearer.

How, to receive me she was at the door
And step by step from there on gave me bliss.
How after that last kiss she came once more
And planted on my lips the *lastest* kiss:
So clear and living does her image rest
With flaming outlines in my loyal breast.

My breast that firmly, like a parapet,
Lives but for her and keeps her locked within,
For her rejoicing that 'tis living yet,
And only knows it lives when she is seen,
And feels more freedom as a willing thrall,
Pulsing alone to thank her for it all.

When my ability to love, when need
Of love requited fades and melts away,
Then hopeful zest for happy hours is freed
For resolutions, deeds without delay!
If ever love inspirits lover's breast,
Most charmingly in me 'tis manifest;

And all through her! What secret fears abounded
And weighed down mind and flesh with heaviness,
And frightful images my vision hounded,
To desolate my sick heart's emptiness;
But now before a well-known threshold nears
New hope, as in soft sunlight she appears.

To God's own peace which here beyond compare
Gives bliss more deep than reason—so 'tis spoke—
I'd liken peace that comes from love so rare
As love which this dear creature can evoke;
There rests the heart, and nothing can dismay
The firm resolve to make me hers for ay.

In unsers Busens Reine wogt ein Streben,
Sich einem Höhern, Reinern, Unbekannten
Aus Dankbarkeit freiwillig hinzugeben,
Enträtselnd sich den ewig Ungenannten;
Wir heissen's: fromm sein!—Solcher seligen Höhe
Fühl' ich mich teilhaft, wenn ich vor ihr stehe.

Vor ihrem Blick, wie vor der Sonne Walten,
Vor ihrem Atem, wie vor Frühlingslüften,
Zerschmilzt, so längst sich eisig starr gehalten,
Der Selbstsinn tief in winterlichen Grüften;
Kein Eigennutz, kein Eigenwille dauert,
Vor ihrem Kommen sind sie weggeschauert.

Es ist, als wenn sie sagte: „Stund' um Stunde
Wird uns das Leben freundlich dargeboten.
Das Gestrige liess uns geringe Kunde,
Das Morgende—zu wissen ist's verboten!
Und wenn ich je mich vor dem Abend scheute,
Die Sonne sank und sah noch, was mich freute.

„Drum tu wie ich und schaue, froh verständig,
Dem Augenblick ins Auge! Kein Verschieben!
Begegn' ihm schnell, wohlwollend wie lebendig,
Im Handeln sei's zur Freude, sei's dem Lieben!
Nur wo du bist, sei alles, immer kindlich,
So bist du alles, bist unüberwindlich."

Du hast gut reden, dacht' ich: zum Geleite
Gab dir ein Gott die Gunst des Augenblickes,
Und jeder fühlt an deiner holden Seite
Sich Augenblicks den Günstling des Geschickes;
Mich schreckt der Wink, von dir mich zu entfernen—
Was hilft es mir, so hohe Weisheit lernen!

Nun bin ich fern! Der jetzigen Minute,
Was ziemt denn der? Ich wüsst' es nicht zu sagen.
Sie bietet mir zum Schönen manches Gute;
Das lastet nur, ich muss mich ihm entschlagen.
Mich treibt umher ein unbezwinglich Sehnen,
Da bleibt kein Rat als grenzenlose Tränen.

So quellt denn fort und fliesset unaufhaltsam—
Doch nie geläng's, die innre Glut zu dämpfen!

In our pure bosom is a striving sown
To give ourselves in gratitude unbidden
To someone higher, purer, here unknown,
Unriddling for ourselves Him ever hidden;
We call it worship!—I can feel the essence
Of such high bliss when I am in her presence.

Under her glance, as when the sun prevails,
Before her breath, as when spring zephyrs come,
All self-love, long confined in icy dales,
Will melt where once it had a wintry home;
No selfish wilfulness can then hold out,
When she appears, 'twill all be put to rout.

It is as though she'd spoken: "Hour by hour
We're offered life—in friendliness 'tis bidden.
The yesterday left us but little dower,
And of the morrow what we'd know, is hidden.
And when the evening ever made me fearful,
The sinking sun still saw why I was cheerful.

"Hence do as I, with cheer be sensible
And face the moment, putting off no deed!
Meet time head on, show vigor, show good will,
In action, if to joy or loving keyed;
Where you are, shape your world, be childlike ever,
You'll be a whole world then and vanquished never."

'Tis well for you to talk, I thought, to guide you
Some god made you the darling of the day,
And each one feels when he is there beside you
That he is fortune's favorite straightway;
The hint that I must leave you gives me fright,
Of what avail is such high wisdom's light?

Now I am gone! And for the present minute
What would be fitting? That I could not say;
I see rich promises of beauty in it,
They're burdensome, and I must keep away;
I'm driven by an overwhelming yearning,
My only refuge, tears forever burning.

Well ever forth and flow unchecked each hour;
This inner fire, though, I could not smother!

Schon rast's und reisst in meiner Brust gewaltsam,
Wo Tod und Leben grausend sich bekämpfen.
Wohl Kräuter gäb's, des Körpers Qual zu stillen;
Allein dem Geist fehlt's am Entschluss und Willen,

    Fehlt's am Begriff: wie sollt' er sie vermissen?
Er wiederholt ihr Bild zu tausend Malen.
Das zaudert bald, bald wird es weggerissen,
Undeutlich jetzt und jetzt im reinsten Strahlen.
Wie könnte dies geringstem Troste frommen,
Die Ebb' und Flut, das Gehen wie das Kommen?

*

    Verlasst mich hier, getreue Weggenossen,
Lasst mich allein am Fels, in Moor und Moos!
Nur immer zu! euch ist die Welt erschlossen,
Die Erde weit, der Himmel hehr und gross;
Betrachtet, forscht, die Einzelheiten sammelt,
Naturgeheimnis werde nachgestammelt.

    Mir ist das All, ich bin mir selbst verloren,
Der ich noch erst den Göttern Liebling war;
Sie prüften mich, verliehen mir Pandoren,
So reich an Gütern, reicher an Gefahr;
Sie drängten mich zum gabeseligen Munde,
Sie trennen mich—und richten mich zu Grunde.

(7) 3. Aussöhnung

    Die Leidenschaft bringt Leiden!—Wer beschwichtigt
Beklommnes Herz, das allzuviel verloren?
Wo sind die Stunden, überschnell verflüchtigt?
Vergebens war das Schönste dir erkoren!
Trüb ist der Geist, verworren das Beginnen;
Die hehre Welt, wie schwindet sie den Sinnen!

    Da schwebt hervor Musik mit Engelschwingen,
Verflicht zu Millionen Tön' um Töne,
Des Menschen Wesen durch und durch zu dringen,
Zu überfüllen ihn mit ew'ger Schöne:
Das Auge netzt sich, fühlt im höhern Sehnen
Den Götterwert der Töne wie der Tränen.

The storm within my breast has gained in power,
Where death and life are warring with each other.
I know of herbs to still the body's ill,
My spirit though lacks all resolve and will,

    Lacks even the thought: how could it miss her ever?
Her image looms a thousand times a day.
It wavers now, and now 'tis gone forever,
Now indistinct, now clear in every ray;
Could any solace from such source be flowing,
The ebb and flow, the coming and the going?

*

    O leave me here, companions good and true,
Leave me alone on cliff, in moss and croft.
Pursue your way! The world's not closed to you,
The earth is wide; high, great is heaven's loft;
Study, observe, cull specimens you see,
Recounting nature's secrets falteringly.

    I've lost the Universe, I'm lost to me,
Lately a darling of the gods in aught;
They tested me, loaned me Pandora free
With blessings rich, with richer dangers fraught;
Toward lips that gladly gave me bliss they urged me,
Now sunder me—and with destruction scourge me.

(7) 3. Reconciliation

    With passion suffering comes. Who can allay
A heart that's lost too much and feels oppressed?
Where are the hours, too quickly flown away?
In vain were you selected for the best!
Clouded the spirit and by plans distraught;
The lofty world has vanished into naught.

    On wings of angels music comes to you,
Weaving a million sweet, harmonious sounds,
To penetrate man's being through and through,
To shower deathless beauty without bounds:
The eye grows moist and feels with longing glow
The heavenly worth of sounds and tears that flow.

Und so das Herz erleichtert merkt behende,
Dass es noch lebt und schlägt und möchte schlagen,
Zum reinsten Dank der überreichen Spende
Sich selbst erwidernd willig darzutragen.
Da fühlte sich—o dass es ewig bliebe!—
Das Doppelglück der Töne wie der Liebe.

8-20. SPRÜCHE

8.   Nehmt nur mein Leben hin in Bausch
Und Bogen, wie ichs führe;
Andre verschlafen ihren Rausch,
Meiner steht auf dem Papiere.

* * *

9.   „Die Feinde, sie bedrohen dich,
Das mehrt von Tag zu Tage sich;
Wie dir doch gar nicht graut!"
Das seh ich alles unbewegt,
Sie zerren an der Schlangenhaut,
Die jüngst ich abgelegt.
Und ist die nächste reif genung,
Ab streif ich die sogleich
Und wandle neubelebt und jung
Im frischen Götterreich.

* * *

10.   „Was willst du, dass von deiner Gesinnung
Man dir nach ins Ewige sende?"
Er gehörte zu keiner Innung,
Blieb Liebhaber bis ans Ende.

* * *

Demut

11.   Seh ich die Werke der Meister an,
So seh ich das, was sie getan;
Betracht ich meine Siebensachen,
Seh ich, was ich hätt sollen machen.

And so the heart is lightened, knowing soon:
It lives and beats and craves to be enduring,
With gratitude for this exuberant boon
Offering itself, requital full assuring.
I felt—o would it ever be like this! —
Of music and of love the twofold bliss.

8-20. EPIGRAMS

8. Accept my life in a single chunk,
   Just as I live and caper;
   Some sleep it off when they are drunk,
   My jag is recorded on paper.

* * *

9. "Your many enemies beset you,
   Yes, more and more each day they fret you,
   And still how calm you've been!"
   I see it, but am not rebuffed;
   They're tugging at a reptile's skin
   Which recently I've sloughed.
   And when a new skin's ripely worn
   I slough it on the sod
   And walk as though but newly born
   Where treads the living God.

* * *

10. "Of all your convictions, what have you willed
    To follow you into eternity?"
    He was never a member of any guild
    And remained an amateur constantly.

* * *

Humility

11. When the works of the masters meet my eye
    Their great achievements before me lie;
    Then, seeing the odds and ends I've spun,
    I realize what I should have done.

* * *

12. Es liesse sich alles trefflich schlichten,
    Könnte man die Sachen zweimal verrichten.

* * *

13. Nicht grössern Vorteil wüsst ich zu nennen,
    Als des Feindes Verdienst erkennen.

* * *

14. Wär nicht das Auge sonnenhaft,
    Die Sonne könnt es nie erblicken;
    Läg nicht in uns des Gottes eigne Kraft,
    Wie könnt uns Göttliches entzücken?

* * *

15. Halte dich nur im stillen rein
    Und lass es um dich wettern;
    Je mehr du fühlst, ein Mensch zu sein,
    Desto ähnlicher bist du den Göttern.

* * *

16. Ein alter Mann ist stets ein König Lear!—
    Was Hand in Hand mitwirkte, stritt,
    Ist längst vorbeigegangen;
    Was mit und an dir liebte, litt,
    Hat sich wo anders angehangen.
    Die Jugend ist um ihretwillen hier,
    Es wäre törig, zu verlangen:
    Komm, ältele du mit mir.

* * *

17. Hör auf doch mit Weisheit zu prahlen, zu prangen,
    Bescheidenheit würde dir löblicher stehn:
    Kaum hast du die Fehler der Jugend begangen,
    So musst du die Fehler des Alters begehn.

* * *

Genug

18. Immer niedlich, immer heiter,
    Immer lieblich! und so weiter,

* * *

12.   To solve our problems it would be nice
If we could but attack them twice.

* * *

13.   No greater advantage could I ferret
Than to recognize an enemy's merit.

* * *

14.   Were eyes, like sun, not luminous,
No sunlight could they ever capture;
If God's own power and strength were not in us,
How could divine things give us rapture?

* * *

15.   Stay clean as quietly as you can,
Let storms rage mightily;
The more you feel that you're a man,
The more like the gods you will be.

* * *

16.   An old man always shares King Lear's plight!
Those toiling, struggling with him, hand in hand,
Have long ago gone by;
Those loving, suffering with and for a friend
Have found some other newer tie.
Just for its own sake youth is with us here.
It would be foolish then to cry:
Come, age with me, my dear!

* * *

17.   Stop boasting of wisdom that you've acquired,
Let modesty abound around you.
From the faults of youth you've barely retired
And already old age and its failings hound you.

* * *

Enough

18.   Always dainty, not woebegone,
Always lovely, and so on,

Stets natürlich, aber klug;
Nun das, dächt' ich, wär' genug.

* * *

19. Hast du es so lange wie ich getrieben,
Versuche wie ich das Leben zu lieben.

* * *

20. Macht's einander nur nicht sauer,
Hier sind wir gleich, Baron und Bauer.

21. FREIBEUTER

Mein Haus hat kein' Tür,
Mein' Tür hat ke Haus;
Und immer mit Schätzel
Hinein und heraus.

Mei Küch hat ke Herd,
Mei Herd hat ke Küch;
Da bratet's und siedet's
Für sich und für mich.

Mei Bett hat ke G'stell,
Mei G'stell hat ke Bett.
Doch wüsst ich nit enen
Der's lustiger hett.

Mei Keller is hoch,
Mei Scheuer is tief,
Zu oberst zu unterst—
Da lag ich und schlief.

Und bin ich erwachen,
Da geht es so fort;
Mei Ort hat ke Bleibens,
Mein Bleibens ken Ort.

22. JAHR AUS JAHR EIN

Ohne Schrittschuh und Schellengeläut
Ist der Januar ein böses Heut.

Ohne Fastnachtstanz und Mummenspiel
Ist am Februar auch nicht viel.

Always natural but wise:
Well, I'd say that would suffice.

* * *

19. Engaged as long as I in toil and strife,
You'll try like me to love and cherish life.

* * *

20. Don't make your neighbor's life unpleasant,
Here we're alike, baron and peasant.

21. FREEBOOTER

My home has no door,
My door has no home,
And always with sweetheart
I go and I come.

My kitchen lacks hearth,
And no kitchen you see,
There's roasting and boiling
For it and for me.

My cot has no frame,
My frame has no cot,
But I know not a soul
With a happier lot.

My cellar is high,
My granary deep,
Up high and down low
I lay there asleep.

And when I'm awoken,
So goes it apace,
In my place I can't stay,
And to stay I've no place

22. YEAR OUT, YEAR IN

Without our skates and sleighbells' **chime**
January's an evil time.

Without carnival dance and mummers' **sport**
February's a trifling sort.

Willst du den März nicht ganz verlieren,
So lass nicht in April dich führen.

Den ersten April musst überstehn,
Dann kann dir manches Guts geschehn.

Und weiterhin im Mai, wenn's glückt,
Hat dich wieder ein Mädchen berückt.

Und das beschäftigt dich so sehr,
Zählst Tage, Wochen und Monde nicht mehr.

23. DÄMMRUNG SENKTE SICH VON OBEN

Dämmrung senkte sich von oben,
Schon ist alle Nähe fern;
Doch zuerst emporgehoben
Holden Lichts der Abendstern!
Alles schwankt ins Ungewisse,
Nebel schleichen in die Höh;
Schwarzvertiefte Finsternisse
Widerspiegelnd ruht der See.

Nun im östlichen Bereiche
Ahn ich Mondenglanz und -Glut,
Schlanker Weiden Haargezweige
Scherzen auf der nächsten Flut.
Durch bewegter Schatten Spiele
Zittert Lunas Zauberschein,
Und durchs Auge schleicht die Kühle
Sänftigend ins Herz hinein.

24. DER BRÄUTIGAM

Um Mitternacht, ich schlief, im Busen wachte
Das liebevolle Herz, als wär es Tag;
Der Tag erschien, mir war, als ob es nachte—
Was ist es mir, so viel er bringen mag?

Sie fehlte ja! mein emsig Tun und Streben,
Für sie allein ertrug ichs durch die Glut
Der heissen Stunde; welch erquicktes Leben
Am kühlen Abend! lohnend wars und gut.

Lest March you lose, make this your rule:
Let folk not brand you an April fool.

When the first of April you've withstood,
You may enjoy a wealth of good.

And again in May, if Luck has called,
By another girl you'll be enthralled.

And she will busy you so much more,
Days, weeks, and months you will ignore.

23. TWILIGHT FROM ABOVE WAS LOWERED

Twilight from above was lowered,
What was near to me is far;
First to loom aloft high-towered
Is the gentle evening star!
Everything is vaguely swaying,
Mists are stealing up on high;
On the lake, at rest, is playing
Blackness mirrored from the sky.

In the east I sense the splendor
Of the moonlight all aglow,
Hairy arms of willows slender
Jest upon the flood below.
Through the play of shadows moving
Trembles Luna's magic art,
Through my eye the coolness roving
Steals with soothing to my heart.

24. THE BETROTHED

At midnight as I slept my love-filled heart
Was waking in my breast as if 'twere day;
Day came—to me 'twas night that would not part—
Its many gifts my grief cannot allay.

I missed her! All my zealousness and strife,
For her alone I bore it through the flood
Of heated hours; o what refreshed new life
In evening's cool! Rewarding 'twas and good.

Die Sonne sank, und Hand in Hand verpflichtet
Begrüssten wir den letzten Segensblick,
Und Auge sprach, ins Auge klar gerichtet:
Von Osten, hoffe nur, sie kommt zurück.

Um Mitternacht, der Sterne Glanz geleitet
Im holden Traum zur Schwelle, wo sie ruht.
O sei auch mir dort auszuruhn bereitet!
Wie es auch sei, das Leben, es ist gut.

25. VERMÄCHTNIS

Kein Wesen kann zu Nichts zerfallen!
Das Ew'ge regt sich fort in allen,
Am Sein erhalte dich beglückt!
Das Sein ist ewig: denn Gesetze
Bewahren die lebend'gen Schätze,
Aus welchen sich das All geschmückt.

Das Wahre war schon längst gefunden,
Hat edle Geisterschaft verbunden:
Das alte Wahre, fass' es an!,
Verdank' es, Erden-Sohn, dem Weisen,
Der ihr, die Sonne zu umkreisen,
Und dem Geschwister wies die Bahn.

Sofort nun wende dich nach innen:
Das Zentrum findest du da drinnen,
Woran kein Edler zweifeln mag.
Wirst keine Regel da vermissen,
Denn das selbständige Gewissen
Ist Sonne deinem Sittentag.

Den Sinnen hast du dann zu trauen:
Kein Falsches lassen sie dich schauen,
Wenn dein Verstand dich wach erhält.
Mit frischem Blick bemerke freudig
Und wandle, sicher wie geschmeidig,
Durch Auen reichbegabter Welt.

Geniesse mässig Füll' und Segen;
Vernunft sei überall zugegen,
Wo Leben sich des Lebens freut.
Dann ist Vergangenheit beständig,

The sun sank low, with hands clasped she and I
Greeted his final glance that blesses men,
And eye declared, as clear it turned to eye:
Have hope, he'll rise up from the East again.

At midnight starry splendor bids me face
In happy dreams the threshold where she stood.
O let me too find respite in that place!
Living, however it may be, is good.

25. LEGACY

What is, cannot reduce to naught!
Th' Eternal lives and breathes in aught—
In what exists, find happiness.
Existence thrives for ay; law measures
And safeguards all the living treasures
With which the Cosmos decked its dress.

Truth had already long been found,
By which great souls were linked and bound;
Let's grasp this age-old truth by force!
Thanks to that Sage do mortals owe
Who bade earth round the sun to go,
And showed earth's sisters all their course.

Turn inward now this very minute,
You'll find the center resting in it,
Which no good man doubts wilfully.
All rules, you'll see, are present here:
A conscience self-reliant, clear,
Sheds light on your morality.

Your senses then you'll have to trust,
They'll let you see what's true and just,
Should reason keep your mind awake.
Observe with sparkling eyes and blithely,
And tread with confidence and lithely
The earth that's rich in field and brake.

Enjoy your boons in moderation,
Let reason have predomination,
Where life delights alive to be.
The past will then be firm and steady,

Das Künftige voraus lebendig—
Der Augenblick ist Ewigkeit.

Und war es endlich dir gelungen,
Und bist du vom Gefühl durchdrungen:
Was fruchtbar ist, allein ist wahr—
Du prüfst das allgemeine Walten,
Es wird nach seiner Weise schalten,
Geselle dich zur kleinsten Schar.

Und wie von alters her, im stillen,
Ein Liebewerk nach eignem Willen
Der Philosoph, der Dichter schuf,
So wirst du schönste Gunst erzielen:
Denn edlen Seelen vorzufühlen
Ist wünschenswertester Beruf.

26. ZUR LOGENFEIER DES DRITTEN SEPTEMBERS 1825

Zwischengesang

Lasst fahren hin das allzu Flüchtige!
Ihr sucht bei ihm vergebens Rat;
In dem Vergangenen lebt das Tüchtige,
Verewigt sich in schöner Tat.

Und so gewinnt sich das Lebendige
Durch Folg' aus Folge neue Kraft,
Denn die Gesinnung die beständige
Sie macht allein den Menschen dauerhaft.

So löst sich jene grosse Frage
Nach unserm zweiten Vaterland;
Denn das Beständige der ird'schen Tage
Verbürgt uns ewigen Bestand.

27. SCHWEBENDER GENIUS ÜBER DER ERDKUGEL

Zwischen oben, zwischen unten
Schweb ich hin zu muntrer Schau,
Ich ergötze mich am Bunten,
Ich erquicke mich im Blau.

The future take on life already—
The moment be eternity.

And when at last success awaits you
And this high feeling penetrates you
That fruitful things alone are true—
You'll test the common motive forces
And find they take their natural courses.
The smallest group is best for you.

Since earliest times, in solitude,
To tasks of love that they deemed good
Wise men and poets were inspired;
So you'll reach favor's fairest goals:
Anticipating noble souls
Is work most ardently desired.

26. ON THE LODGE CELEBRATION OF SEPTEMBER 3, 1825

Interlude

Discard what's all-too-transitory!
'Twill give no counsel in your need:
Achievement lives in ancient story,
Grows deathless now in noble deed.

And so what lives and what is thriving
Through cause and action gains new force,
For constancy of mind and striving
Alone give man a fixed, enduring course.

This solves the great interrogation:
Where may our second homeland be?
For what we do on earth that has duration
Vouchsafes us our eternity.

27. HOVERING GENIUS OVER THE EARTH-SPHERE

Pointing upward and below,
I hover for a happy view,
Charmed by all the colors' glow,
I find refreshment in the blue.

Und wenn mich am Tag die Ferne
Luftiger Berge sehnlich zieht,
Nachts das Übermass der Sterne
Prächtig mir zu Häupten glüht—

Alle Tag' und alle Nächte
Rühm ich so des Menschen Los;
Denkt er ewig sich ins Rechte,
Ist er ewig schön und gross.

When in daytime distant regions
Lure my dreams to wind-swept heights,
And at nighttime stars in legions
Over me shed glorious light—

Day or night, it matters never,
I will praise man's earthly fate;
Thinking righteous thought, forever
He'll have beauty, he'll be great.

Index of Titles and First Lines

Ach! unaufhaltsam strebet das Schiff, 52
Alexander und Cäsar ..., 46
Alexis und Dora, 52
Antepirrhema, 96
An Werther, 98
Auf Kieseln im Bache ..., 18
Aussöhnung, 108

Dämmrung senkte sich von oben, 116
Da sind sie nun! ..., 18
Dem Geier gleich, 32
Demut, 110
Der Bräutigam, 116
Die Welt durchaus ist lieblich anzuschauen, 90
Die Braut von Korinth, 60
Die Feinde, sie bedrohen dich, 110
Die Leidenschaft bringt Leiden ..., 108
Die Liebende abermals, 70
Diese Gondel vergleich ich ..., 46

Ein alter Mann ist stets ein König Lear, 112
Ein Blumenglöckchen, 72
Ein Strom entrauscht umwölktem Felsensaale, 70
Ein unverschämter Naseweis, 74
Elegie, 100
Epigramme. Venedig 5, 46
Epigramme. Venedig 8, 46
Epigramme. Venedig 10, 48
Epigramme. Venedig 96, 48
Epirrhema, 96
Epoche, 71
Er, der einzige Gerechte, 82
Es ist ein Schnee gefallen, 78
Es liesse sich alles trefflich schlichten, 112

Freibeuter, 114
Freudig war, vor vielen Jahren, 96

Genug, 112
Gesteht's! die Dichter des Orients, 82
Glänzen sah ich das Meer ..., 48
Gleich und gleich, 72
Gott sandte seinen rohen Kindern, 74

Halte dich nur im stillen rein, 112
Harzreise im Winter, 32
Hast du es so lange wie ich getrieben, 114
Hatem, 84
Heiss mich nicht reden ..., 40
Herrin, sag! was heisst das Flüstern?, 90

Hör' auf doch mit Weisheit zu prahlen, zu prangen, 112
Ich komme bald ..., 20
Immer niedlich, immer heiter, 112
In der Gondel lag ich gestreckt ..., 46
In welchem Weine?, 92
Ist es möglich? Stern der Sterne, 86

Jahr aus Jahr ein, 114

Kein Wesen kann zu nichts zerfallen, 118
Krittler, 74

Lasst fahren hin das allzu Flüchtige, 120
Locken, haltet mich ..., 84

Mächtiges Überraschen, 70
Macht's einander nur nicht sauer, 114
Mahomets Gesang, 28
Manche Töne sind mir Verdruss ..., 46
März, 78
Mein Haus hat kein' Tür, 114
Mignon 1, 40
Mignon 2, 40
Mit Flammenschrift war innigst eingeschrieben, 72
Müsset im Naturbetrachten, 96

Nach Korinthus von Athen gezogen, 60
Nach Mittage sassen wir ..., 20
Nehmt nur mein Leben hin in Bausch, 110
Nicht grössern Vorteil wüsst' ich zu nennen, 112
Nimmer will ich dich verlieren, 86
Noch einmal wagst du, vielbeweinter Schatten, 98

Ob ich Irdsches denk' und sinne, 82
Ohne Schrittschuh und Schellengeläut, 114

Parabase, 96
Philine, 40
Poesie, 74

Römische Elegie X, 46
Römische Elegie XVII, 46

Schwebender Genius über der Erdkugel, 120
Seh' ich die Werke der Meister an, 110
Seht den Felsenquell, 28

Singet nicht in Trauertönen, 40
So lasst mich scheinen . . ., 40
Soll man dich nicht aufs schmählichste berauben, 82
So schauet mit bescheidnem Blick, 96
Sprüche, 110
Stirbt der Fuchs . . ., 20
Suleika 1, 82
Suleika, 2, 86
Suleika 3, 86

Talismane, 82
Trilogie der Leidenschaft, 98

Ultimatum, 98
Um Mitternacht, ich schlief . . ., 116
Und so sag' ich zum letzten Male, 98
Urworte. Orphisch, 74

Vermächtnis, 118
Volk und Knecht und Überwinder, 82
Vollmondnacht, 90

Wanderers Sturmlied, 22
Wär nicht das Auge sonnenhaft, 112
Warum ich wieder zum Papier mich wende?, 70
Warum treibt sich das Volk so . . ., 48
Was bedeutet die Bewegung?, 86
Was soll ich nun vom Wiedersehen hoffen, 100
Was willst du, dass von deiner Gesinnung, 110
Wechsel, 18
Wen du nicht verlässest . . ., 22
Wenn der schwer Gedrückte klagt, 82
Wie an dem Tag, der dich der Welt verliehen, 74
Wiederfinden, 86

Zueignung, 18
Zur Logenfeier des Dritten Septembers 1825. Zwischengesang, 120
Zwischen oben, zwischen unten, 120

www.ingramcontent.com/pod-product-compliance
Lightning Source LLC
Chambersburg PA
CBHW031316150426
43191CB00005B/259